C000181635

Candlestick Charts

An introduction to using candlestick charts

Clive Lambert

HARRIMAN HOUSE LTD
3A Penns Road
Petersfield
Hampshire
GU32 2EW
GREAT BRITAIN

Tel: +44 (0)1730 233870
Fax: +44 (0)1730 233880
Email: enquiries@harriman-house.com
Website: www.harriman-house.com

First published in Great Britain in 2009 by Harriman House.

Copyright © Harriman House Ltd

The right of Clive Lambert to be identified as the author has been asserted in accordance with the Copyright, Design and Patents Act 1988.

ISBN 978-1-905641-74-1

British Library Cataloguing in Publication Data

A CIP catalogue record for this book can be obtained from the British Library.

All rights reserved; no part of this publication may be reproduced, stored in a retrieval system, or transmitted in any form or by any means, electronic, mechanical, photocopying, recording, or otherwise without the prior written permission of the Publisher. This book may not be lent, resold, hired out or otherwise disposed of by way of trade in any form of binding or cover other than that in which it is published without the prior written consent of the Publisher.

Charts provided courtesy of CQG, Inc.

Printed in the UK by the MPG Books Group

No responsibility for loss occasioned to any person or corporate body acting or refraining to act as a result of reading material in this book can be accepted by the Publisher, by the Author, or by the employer of the Author.

Contents

Preface

Who this book is for

In this book I aim to introduce candlestick analysis to anyone from an absolute beginner to an experienced market professional who has a working knowledge of charting. The language should be simple enough for a novice, but shouldn't exclude those with more experience, as my aim is to change your viewing of a candlestick chart into a search for the answer to the perennial question "Who's controlling the market: the bulls or the bears?" Ideally, you will have some knowledge of the markets, and even more ideally you will be a cynic about technical analysis, and this book will convert you!

What the book covers

After a brief introduction I will spend a good deal of time looking at three very different basic shapes of candlestick to get a firm grip on the principles involved.

Then I will take a more broad-brush approach to cover several other patterns that can signify reversals or continuations of trend, focusing particularly on the powerful reversal patterns.

In later chapters I will expand on several aspects of candlestick analysis and their uses in practical trading situations. Candlesticks can be used over different time frames and we will look at their application whether you are a short-term trader or a long-term money manager. I will end by explaining how candles can be used for entering and exiting trades when used in conjunction with support and resistance levels as well as with other basic forms of technical analysis such as momentum indicators.

The book does not go into the more esoteric forms of candlestick charting – there are a wide variety of advanced candlestick patterns that can take years to learn – nor does it cover hybrid methods such as Ichimoku charting, which is a subject in itself. However, close study of this book should enable anyone to use candlesticks in their analysis of the markets, and improve their trading and decision-making.

Foreword

The human mind is not as good at processing large amounts of information as we might like. Psychologists have shown that human beings are only able to juggle small numbers of related and often conflicting pieces of information without making judgement errors. As a result, individuals faced with the vast amounts of information available to support investment decisions often find themselves swamped by the enormity of the task; unable to see the wood from the trees.

Technical analysis is a field of financial markets research that works to address the above problem by focusing on a single, universally available, data source that reflects all known information and activity relating to all financial securities. Price history.

Technical analysts argue that as markets are efficient, prices reflect all known information and that they move over time as participants react to new information and changing needs. As a result, the technical analysis of these price changes can provide real insight into the market dynamics and be used to develop trading strategies that exhibit superior risk/reward characteristics.

Technical analysts use price history to show them what market participants are doing with their money. By tracking prices they can develop an understanding of the market's own psychology and identify patterns of behaviour that are frequently repeated. Technical analysis is used to create trading strategies that are both objective and efficient. Entry and exit prices can be identified in advance and subsequent price data can be employed as an instantaneous feedback mechanism for trade management and strategy refinement. In this way, technical analysis greatly assists in distilling the vast amounts of conflicting and complex information available to develop winning investment strategies.

While technical analysis approaches have developed significantly over the past few decades, some techniques are far more ancient. While their real origins are unknown, Japanese candlestick charts have been recorded as being employed in the rice markets as far back as the 1600s. What is particularly interesting is that many of these ancient approaches continue to provide highly effective trading signals when applied to modern markets and securities. For this reason, it's no surprise perhaps that candlestick charting techniques are so extensively employed by the world's most professional investors.

Clive Lambert is one of the UK's leading experts in the use and application of Japanese candlestick chart analysis. I have known him for many years and have learnt to greatly respect his depth of knowledge and the objectiveness it brings to his market strategies.

In this book, Clive has combined his love of the subject with his experience as a professional trader, to demystify candlestick charting and make it accessible and effective for the reader. His writing style is conversational and his explanations clear and practical. As a result, the book is a refreshing departure from the dry and complex writing often associated with financial markets. With insight and clarity, the book unravels the psychology behind price patterns and provides a powerful collection of simple and effective methods to trade for profit and control risk.

For all the above reasons, I am happy to recommend this book and proud to have been asked to write this foreword. Investing in financial markets is notoriously hazardous and no technique, however clever, is infallible. However, candlestick charts provide a powerful set of analytical tools designed to maximise profits and minimise losses in the business of financial markets trading. These tools are invaluable for all those seeking to make their fortune in the markets and this book is an excellent way to learn about many of them.

Adam Sorab
Chairman – Society of Technical Analysts (STA) 1998-2008
Director – International Federation of Technical Analysis Societies (IFTA)

Introduction

My personal journey with technical analysis and candles

Stock Exchange Floor to LIFFE Floor (via Sydney)

My first experience of technical analysis was at my very first job in the City, fresh out of school, listening to Robin Griffiths on the fifth floor of the offices of the stockbrokers James Capel as a wide-eyed 16-year-old kid. I remember thinking that he seemed to make a lot more sense than many of the "fundamentalists" who took the microphone. His longevity and continued high standing in the industry is proof of the pudding.

My next experience came four years later, on my first day in the 90-Day Bank Bills booth for the brokers Tullett and Tokyo on the Sydney Futures Exchange. I was given the point & figure chart to keep up to date: a collection of pieces of graph paper, taped together, which in its unfolded state stretched across several metres. Many a fellow (older!) technician that I come across these days had a similar first experience. Ah, those were the days!

Soon after that I had the privilege of working on the LIFFE Floor for a total of ten years, both at the Royal Exchange (now the site of a few rather swanky shops and restaurants) and at Cannon Bridge (where LIFFE still reside, despite the coloured jackets having long been hung up for the last time, or framed as a memento in the case of a few, mine included). I say it was a privilege because it's truly something to tell the grandchildren, even though we didn't know it at the time. It was just such great fun. It was 100% "work hard, play hard". When there was work to be done, orders to be filled, clients to please, we knuckled down and did a great job. I was there for several major events: Black Wednesday, LTCM, and the fall of Barings, the last of which was very close to home for some floor operatives.

But there was something else that working on the LIFFE Floor did for me personally, something that I didn't even realise at the time would stand me in such good stead for my future career as a technical analyst: it got me into watching price action unfold live.

After leaving LIFFE and starting work in an office, which is when I first started looking at candlestick charts, I realised that I was doing exactly the same thing with technical charts as I used to do on the floor: watching the price action, and making assumptions on the back of what I was seeing. It was an almost seamless transition. I remember my boss mocking me the first time I asked if I could send out some support and resistance levels on the Bloomberg to the client base: 'Ah, so you think you're a technical analyst, do you? Ha ha ha!' Within six months he was dragging me round hedge fund companies getting me to show them the latest Bund chart – how quickly it changed! This was obviously a huge result for me personally, as only months before my attempts to talk about the technicals were merely based on trying to keep my job. My previous floor broking skills – hand signals and shouting loudly – were largely redundant.

I lasted a year or so in the office. Working in a sterile office with just a handful of people was a bit of a culture shock after the Floor. I was also rather tired of the negative tag that was attached to ex-Floor operatives at that time. So my family and I decided to up sticks, move to Australia, and at the same time I set up my own company to sell my technical analysis commentary.

The Australian dream lasted just 16 months before the Lamberts packed up and came back home to England. The company is still going though, and I'm still, eight years on, happily jumping out of bed at the crack of dawn to write about the markets, based mainly on observations from the candlestick charts.

Before I stop talking about myself I'd like to thank my wife Rachael for all her support over the years, and particularly in the months that I spent writing this book. She has been a solid rock and a true friend.

Thank you my love.

Financials to commodities

In recent years my team have been asked to diversify our product base – to look at commodities, metals, equities, and all sorts of other weird and wonderful things. When starting to look at a new market we've done the same thing each and every time. We use the same templates that we've used previously, most of which use a basic canvas of candlestick charts over a range of different time frames. We've always said that if after a few weeks or months this methodology clearly isn't working, we'll have a rethink. So far we've never had to have a rethink, and now have many readers for our daily ramblings across many different markets, all using the markets for different reasons, and all finding a use for our analysis of the candlestick charts.

The Society of Technical Analysts

At the same time as building up the business I have also become heavily involved in the UK Society of Technical Analysts, and I joined the Board of the Society in 2003. I have found this to be an invaluable experience and I feel both privileged and fortunate to have become friends with some of this country's leading analysts. I would like to take this opportunity to thank these people for taking me seriously and giving me the confidence to grow as an analyst to the point where my thoughts are now being put down in print. I would particularly like to thank Adam Sorab, Chairman of the Society from 1998 to 2008, for his enthusiastic support of my work, and for writing the foreword to this book.

1

What Are Candlesticks?

A potted history

Candlesticks have been around a lot longer than anything similar in the Western world. The Japanese were looking at charts as far back as the 17th century, whereas the earliest known charts in the US appeared in the late 19th century. Rice trading had been established in Japan in 1654, with gold, silver and rape seed oil following soon after. Rice markets dominated Japan at this time and the commodity became, it seems, more important than hard currency.

Munehisa Homma (aka Sokyu Honma), a Japanese rice trader born in the early 1700s, is widely credited as being one of the early exponents of tracking price action. He understood basic supply and demand dynamics, but also identified the fact that emotion played a part in the setting of price. He wanted to track the emotion of the market players, and this work became the basis of candlestick analysis. He was extremely well respected, to the point of being promoted to Samurai status.

The Japanese did an extremely good job of keeping candlesticks quiet from the Western world, right up until the 1980s, when suddenly there was a large cross-pollination of banks and financial institutions around the world. This is when Westerners suddenly got wind of these mystical charts. Obviously this was also about the time that charting in general suddenly became a lot easier, due to the widespread use of the PC.

In the late 1980s several Western analysts became interested in candlesticks. In the UK Michael Feeny, who was then head of TA in London for Sumitomo, began using candlesticks in his daily work, and started introducing the ideas to London professionals. In the December 1989 edition of *Futures* magazine Steve Nison, who was a technical analyst at Merrill Lynch in New York, produced a paper that showed a series of candlestick reversal patterns and explained their predictive powers. He went on to write a book on the subject, and a fine book it is too. Thank you Messrs Feeny and Nison.

Since then candlesticks have gained in popularity by the year, and these days they seem to be the standard template that most analysts work from.

I'm going to leave the history lesson there, because unlike other esteemed experts on Japanese charting methods I've never had the privilege of either sitting down with a Japanese expert, nor even going to Japan. So this book, if you like, can be classed as a Westerner's take on an ancient Japanese method.

Because of this I've deliberately avoided spending too much time referring to the Japanese phraseology or the translations.

Construction of candlestick charts

Candlesticks versus traditional bar charts

Until the late 1980s the Western world used bar charts as the standard method for charting the markets. A bar chart displays price on the vertical axis and time along the horizontal axis; each bar represents a set time period (eg, a day or a week or a month). For the moment we'll stick to daily charts. The four pieces of data used in a bar chart are: the day's open, high, low and close. Figure 1-1 shows how these four levels are displayed.

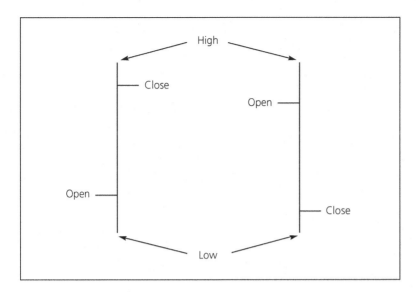

Figure 1-1: Bar chart construction

Candlestick charts use the same price levels as bar charts (ie, open, high, low, close), but they display the data in a different way – as can be seen in the following figure.

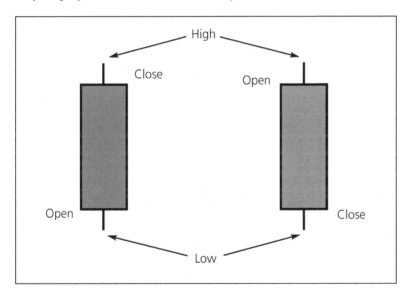

Figure 1-2: Candlestick chart construction

By comparing the bar charts and candlesticks you can see that the principles are similar – they both present in a graphical format the essential price data (open, high, low, close) for a given period.

Let's look at an actual example.

The figure below shows a standard bar chart, while the following figure is the same chart but this time using candlesticks instead of bars.

Source: CQG, Inc. © 2008 All rights reserved worldwide.

Figure 1-3: Bar chart (factual, but uninspiring)

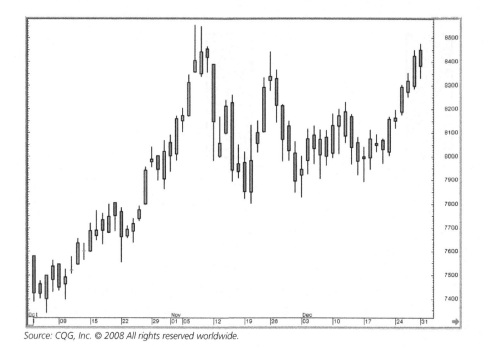

Source: CQG, Inc. © 2008 All rights reserved worldwide.

Figure 1-4: Candlestick chart (factual, and emotive)

By comparing the preceding two charts, you can see that the shape of the charts is the same. (The two charts actually show the price behaviour of gold at the end of 2007 – but it is not important to know that at this stage.)

Although the overall shape of the charts is the same, the candlestick chart is easier to read because the candles do a much better job of clearly distinguishing the exact relationship between the four prices for each period. For example, it is easy to see whether a period was bullish or bearish (by the colour).

Summary

The information carried in bar and candlestick charts is the same, but the design of the latter makes it easier to spot patterns that can be significant to a trader or analyst.

The anatomy of the candles

Let's have a closer look at the colour scheme used in the candlestick charts. A closer inspection of Figure 1-4 shows that the candlesticks are different colours depending on whether the market closed above or below the open. The fat bit in the middle is the difference between the open and the close, and is called the real body of the candlestick.

A candlestick with a green real body is created on a day when the market closed higher than where it opened. In other words price moved higher over the course of the day. This means, if you use the basic principles of supply and demand, there were more buyers than sellers. To put it into the market parlance that I will use from now on, the bulls won the day.

A candlestick with a red real body is the result of a day where the market closed below the level at which it opened. This means the sellers outweighed the buyers, or there was more supply than demand, resulting in price moving lower. In market terms it was a bearish day.

So we now know that the difference between the open and the close is called the real body, and that its colour depends on whether it was a bullish or bearish day, from open to close.

I would stress at this point that the colour of a candlestick is nothing to do with where a market closes in relation to the previous day's close. This is a common mistake that many people make because on quote boards prices are often displayed either as red or green depending on whether the market is higher or lower compared to the previous close.

If, for example, a stock closed at £1.00 yesterday, then opened today at £1.10, but by afternoon trade had sold off to close at £1.03, it would still be up 3 pence on the day. However, the candlestick's real body would be big and red because the stock opened at £1.10 then closed at £1.03.

I have illustrated this in Figure 1-5 below.

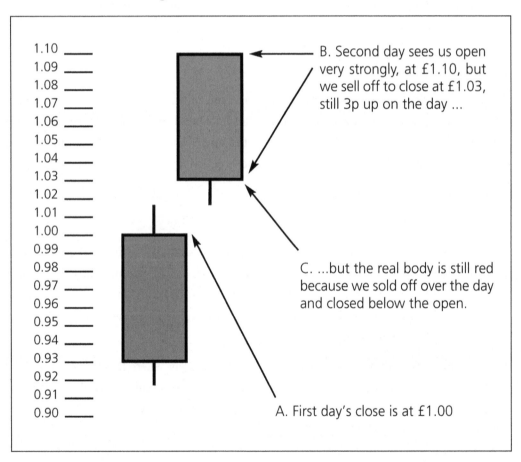

Figure 1-5: Example of a higher close than the previous day's, but still a red candle

Let's finish off this walk through the construction by adding some terminology into the equation.

The figure below shows the other terminology you need to be aware of with respect to the different elements of an individual candlestick.

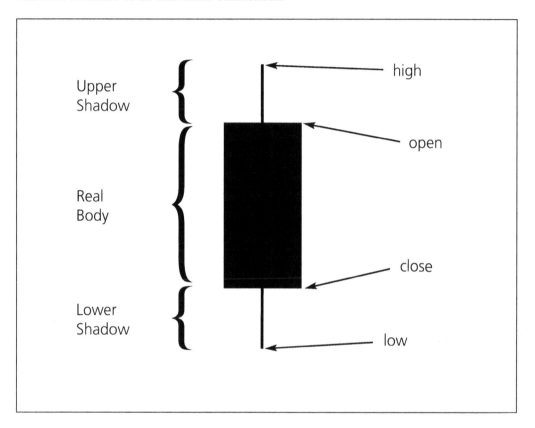

Figure 1-6: Terminology

The difference between the top of the real body and the high of the day is the upper shadow (sometimes called the upper wick).

The difference between the bottom of the real body and the low of the day is the lower shadow (or lower wick).

Another way to think about it is that there's a line all the way down the middle of a candlestick representing the day's range. The Japanese call this the *kage* or the shadow line.

It is important to be happy with these terms as I will continually use them throughout the rest of the book.

The charts I will use throughout this book, for the sake of continuity, are all taken from a charting system called CQG. Their favoured colour scheme, and the one I've grown used to using in my daily routine, is green (for bullish) and red (for bearish) candles, as illustrated so far in this book.

Different charting systems have different default settings, although with most half decent systems you can change the candles to whatever suits you. Just make sure you know which way round they are!

In fact – and confusingly – the Japanese traditionally used red candles for up days and black candles for down days, red being a lucky colour in Japan.

A general rule of thumb that will usually see you right is that solid blocks are down days, whereas real bodies that are light of colour are bullish candles.

This may also help you in case you come across candlestick charts in black and white only.

Again there is a custom that is generally accepted in candlestick analysis, and I will use this for the rest of the book, just to try and keep things standardised:

Open < Close = bullish = light in colour = open real body

Open > Close = bearish = dark in colour = filled real body

The psychology of charts and trading

The idea of a chart in the first place is to illustrate where the price of a security has been. Supply and demand sets the price of something, and the chart is a graphical representation of the historical changes in supply and demand, ie, the historical changes in overall thinking towards the product being viewed, as set by buyers and sellers.

Technical analysis concerns itself with looking for trends in price, and also looking for signs that these trends are ending or reversing. This is something that candlesticks can do much more quickly and much more clearly than most other technical methods.

There are advantages and disadvantages with all types of market analysis, and within technical analysis there are methods that react slowly to changes and therefore don't suit certain types of trader or analyst, whereas there are other methods that give many more signals but tend not to be so robust. Some prefer this. Candlesticks are often put into the latter category.

Later on I will explore how you can add other things to your candlestick analysis to come up with more robust trading ideas.

Overall, the answer is to combine a few things with your candlestick charts so that you come up with a trading strategy that suits your needs and your personality. Some may even decide that they don't need to use candlesticks for a specific strategy, but instead just to give a snapshot view of the market minute-by-minute, day by day, or week by week.

> For now the key thing to understand is that candlesticks are a graphical representation of price movement, and therefore show the market's thinking and sentiment, and any changes in this thinking and sentiment that may be unfolding.

So, technical analysis shows what the market thinks of a stock or security. Obviously the market is the collective mass of people who are trading or investing in any particular instrument. Therefore the price is the definitive proxy of what the market – every type of trader involved, all bundled together into one mass – thinks about that instrument.

> It is people that set price, and people who form the chart. In other words technical analysis is quite simply a study of human behaviour – or psychology to you and me.

And this is what I do with candlesticks: I dig into the psychology of each of the patterns that make up candlestick analysis. There are many different patterns, all with different shapes. In the coming chapters we're going to go through the different patterns, work out what movement in price formed these shapes, and then translate that into the psychology of the market at each step of the formation of the pattern. What was the market thinking that resulted in these particular patterns? And why does this often translate into a reversal or continuation of the trend?

An easy way to think about the market is as if it's a battle between the buyers and the sellers. Just split it into two distinct groups of traders: the bulls and the bears. Obviously this is quite a generalisation, but it can be a very effective way of analysing market movements – maybe because it personalises it.

This is the crux of the whole book, in my opinion. I have tried to help you understand the construction of the different patterns that appear in candlestick charts in order that you can deduce what is happening in the market for yourself. While reading this book, hopefully you will have "a light-bulb moment" and realise what candlesticks can do for you, no matter what you're trying to gain from your charts. I am hoping you will see how candlesticks can help you to answer some of the rather confusing questions I have already posed about market psychology and the minute-by-minute changes in sentiment. Market psychology underpins candlestick analysis, and I have thrown it in at this early stage to get you thinking in this way!

Chapter summary

- You should now be comfortable with the construction of candlesticks, know the names of the component parts, and understand the difference between open and filled real bodies.

- A candlestick with an open (green) real body is the result of a day where the market closes above its opening price, and the open real body is the difference between the open and close.

- A filled (red) real body on a daily candlestick means the market closed below the opening price, and the filled real body is the difference between these two values.

- The line down the middle of any candlestick pattern defines the day's range – the high to low.

- Candlesticks are designed to give you a graphical representation of the market psychology at any given moment.

2

What Candles Tell Us About The State Of Mind Of The Market

Marabuzo v Doji candles

Pattern recognition is a cornerstone of technical analysis. Western practitioners have been spotting things like Dow Theory signals, and all sorts of patterns with names like Rounded Bottom and Head & Shoulders, for years. This is why viewing candlestick charts can be an easy transition for technical analysts, because it's a similar practice: you look for recurring patterns, and use the assumption that price patterns repeat themselves, so similar behaviour will be seen after these price patterns when they occur in the future.

Let's begin our journey into pattern recognition of candlestick charts.

Look at the three candlesticks in the following figure, and in the space next to them jot down what happened to give us such a shaped candle.

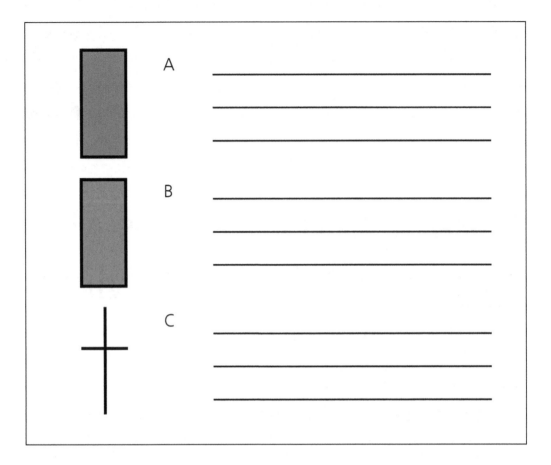

Figure 2-1: Three different candlesticks – your thoughts?

Hopefully you jotted down something along these lines:

In candlestick A the market rallied from the first trade, and closed on the day's high.

In pattern B traders spent all day selling off. The high was the first trade of the day, and the low was the last trade.

In pattern C the market opened and closed at the same price, having tried to move higher then lower (or vice versa) over the course of the day.

The next step is to think about the state of mind of the market on each of these very different sessions, and in turn we can get a feel for market sentiment, at least for that particular session.

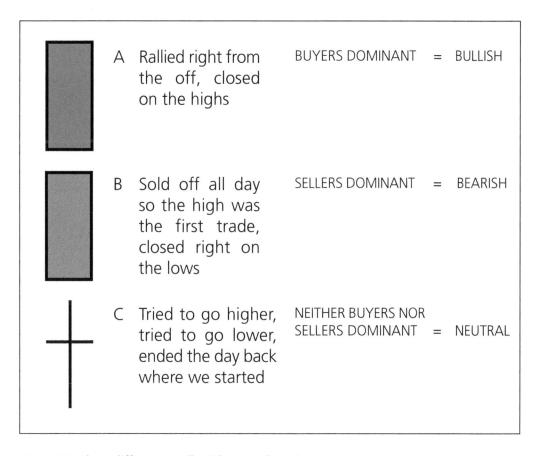

Figure 2-2: Three different candlesticks – my thoughts

Some simple assumptions can now be made. If the buyers were still active on the close of candlestick A, is it likely that they may still want to buy some more tomorrow when the market re-opens? If they were buying as the market closed it could be argued that they haven't finished. It was only the market closing that stopped them from buying more.

If the sellers were active and dominant right up until the last second of trading on candlestick B, are they suddenly going to disappear into the ether when things start again the next day? Unlikely!

On day C no one could make up his or her mind. For a while the bulls were winning, but then the sellers appeared, and the market sold off. But this selling didn't last, and by the close the market was right back where it started. If the buyers and sellers were equal to each other either confusion reigned supreme over the session, or indifference led to a "nothing" day.

Or it could have been an almighty ding-dong dust up between buyers and sellers, but no one won in the end – the equivalent of a boxing match being tied after 12 bruising rounds.

In candlestick analysis most patterns are given a name, and the three patterns we have looked at are no exception.

The first two are sessions where there is a strong push in one direction.

> A candlestick with a long real body and very little in the way of shadows is called a Marabuzo.

Marabuzo is the Japanese word for "shaven head", so it's descriptive of the look of the candlestick; with very little shadow showing up – it definitely can look like a candle that's had a severe haircut!

In my research I've come across a couple of alternative spellings, the most common being Marubozu. I have also come across this being described as "formed with only two prices" which is quite clever, when you look at the formation of these patterns.

> A bullish Marabuzo is a strong conviction day in favour of the buyers: a big open candlestick.
>
> A bearish Marabuzo is a candlestick that's mostly made up of filled real body: bearish domination.

This sort of session is the purest form of continuation pattern, as an assumption can be made (as mentioned earlier) that the market will carry on in the same direction after such a strong conviction day.

Our third candlestick has no real body at all, due to the fact that the market opened and closed at almost exactly the same level.

A candlestick with no (or a very small) real body is known as a Doji.

We will look at the Doji candlestick in more detail in the next chapter, because it is a powerful reversal pattern.

In a strong uptrend the buyers are dominating almost daily. If you suddenly get a Doji day this means the bulls didn't dominate – if you take the day as a whole, they were totally matched by the bears; hence the market ended up back where it started. This is a change from what went on before.

The same can be said for a Doji that appears in a downtrending market: a Doji shows that the bears may be struggling to sustain their push to lower prices, and therefore a reversal may be occurring.

Chapter summary

This is the crux of candlestick analysis: by looking at the shape of any candlestick we can surmise what's happened over that time period. We can then make assumptions on the balance of power between bulls and bears, and on those assumptions decide whether this balance is starting to tip the other way.

Trading and charting the markets can be classed as an exercise in playing the odds. If you can effectively and successfully gauge market direction you are already doing better than merely flicking a coin (which is akin to many people's decision making process!)

Now we'll go through some of the more common and more powerful reversal patterns and work out why they're classed as reversals.

3

Single Reversal Patterns

An in depth look at the Hammer to see why this is a reversal signal, and such a strong one!

Hammer

The first pattern we're going to look at is the Hammer. This is a rare treat in candlestick analysis: a pattern that looks like its name!

A Hammer looks like a hammer, with a small fat head and a long handle.

With every candlestick pattern in the following chapters I'm going to put the set of rules for each pattern in a highlighted box, for easy reference. You may have already noticed the "Cheat Sheet" on the inside covers of this book – this will hopefully become your first point of reference once you've finished reading the main chapters.

Rules

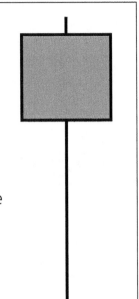

Hammer properties

BULLISH REVERSAL

1. Small real body

2. Real body is at the top end of the day's range

3. Very small, or no upper shadow

4. The long lower shadow should be at least twice the height of the real body

5. The colour of the real body is not important

6. Market is in a **downtrend**

Construction

Let's expand on the above, just to make sure everything's clear. Think about our Doji: this was the result of an open and close at similar levels – an even balance between bulls and bears. The Hammer has a small real body, so with this pattern we have the same thing – a pretty even balance between buyers and sellers. This is also the reason why the colour of the real body isn't important; it's the size of the real body that's important. We'll talk about this a bit more later on.

The small real body is at the top end of the day's range, so there is not much happening above the top of the real body. This leaves us with a lot of lower shadow, and as I've said in the box above this should be at least twice the measurement of the real body. I'm never sure whether to say twice the height or twice the length, but hopefully you've got the idea. Most charting systems have a cursor functionality where you can check the open, high, low and close of the candlestick if you put your cursor over it – you can use this function to check if it qualifies.

The final condition is very important and, unfortunately, often forgotten. Remember we're looking at a reversal pattern here, so the market needs something to reverse. Only if we see this shape of candlestick in a falling market can we call it a Hammer.

There is a name for this shape of candlestick in a rising market (the Hanging Man), but it's not as strong a reversal signal as a Hammer and, anyway, we're going to look at it later on in this chapter.

The fact is, the Hammer is an extremely potent reversal pattern and one of the simplest to understand, which is why we'll spend a bit of time on it. As you can see from the following chart it certainly did a good job in this instance. This was the August 2007 subprime sell-off in the Dow – the first time it hit the fan anyway!

Source: CQG, Inc. © 2008 All rights reserved worldwide.

Figure 3-1: Dow Jones Industrial Average; daily candlestick chart; 10 July 2007 – 20 September 2007, showing 16 August 2007 Hammer

We can see clearly from this chart that the Hammer candlestick did indeed call an end to the selling, and from here the market rallied strongly, only returning to these levels months later.

Getting inside the pattern

Why is a candlestick shaped like this such an important reversal? To answer this question we need to think about the price action that goes into the formation of a candlestick of this shape.

The best way to do this is to zoom in on that particular day and see what actually happened over the session, but while we do this we should also keep in mind that the daily chart only requires four pieces of data: the open, high, low and close on that day.

Below is a 10-minute candle chart for the Dow Jones Industrial Average on 16 August 2007. We have added to the chart the general direction of travel, joining up the day's open, low, high and close.

We have cut the day into small 10-minute segments and the following chart shows the direction of travel taken if we split the price action down into these small parts.

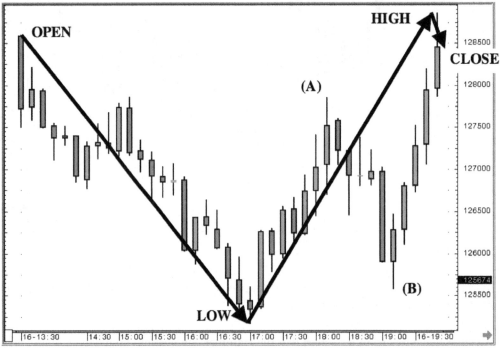

Source: CQG, Inc. © 2008 All rights reserved worldwide.

Figure 3-2: Dow Jones Industrial Average; 10-minute candlestick chart for 16 August 2007

You can see that on this day the market sold off dramatically – over 300 points in the first 4 hours of trade – but then rallied strongly and took back all of the earlier losses, closing the session right back at the highs. What a roller-coaster ride!

So that's what happens on a Hammer day. It's clear as a bell if you look at the previous chart:

> The market sold off sharply, then hit a price where the selling stopped and the buyers took over. From here the market rallied strongly and ended up right back where it started. It also closed near the high, which is important, because quite often a sell off in late trade can spoil the party. But in this case the gains seen in the second half of the session were sustained into the close.

It could have been so different

You can see that the bears had another go in afternoon trade on this particular day – the sell off between the points marked A and B on our chart. But the bulls reacted once more to this weakness and the market rallied late on and closed strongly, leaving us **overall** with a "V" shaped direction of travel.

So a Hammer on the daily chart represents a "V" shaped direction of travel over the course of the day as a whole.

Psychology

Let's think about our bulls and bears and their mindset at each point of the day. At the start when the markets begin to sell off no one is surprised, are they? After all, the market is experiencing some selling off, which is something we're quite used to happening when you consider the market is in a downtrend. Right up until the moment the market hit the low the bears are in charge, and they're probably very pleased with themselves. They've been bossing things of late, and today they're just doing more of the same.

Imagine, with this level of complacency, how uncomfortable the afternoon suddenly becomes for the bears with each tick higher. And they don't get the chance to get out either, because there isn't any pullback on the close to cover positions on. They keep thinking the market's going to fall over again and they can cash in some chips, but this sell-off doesn't come.

The bulls on the other hand, are suddenly feeling empowered, after all they're now having a good day (compared to how they were doing when the market was on the low), which isn't something they've been able to say much of late!

Who goes home happier that night? I think the bulls, because finally they've had a good day. Things are certainly a lot better for them now than they were when the market hit that low earlier in the session.

The bears will have seen their profits diminished; they're not particularly used to this just lately, and they won't like it. They may well stew on it overnight, then come in tomorrow, swallow their pride, and cover their shorts (becoming buyers in the process). They may even decide that if you can't beat them, join them, and they'll become outright bulls.

Hopefully this gives some insight into why this sort of session can be so important and trend changing. A Hammer represents a session where things change. Where the sellers drop the ball, where the buyers suddenly wake up and where the balance of power shifts from the sellers to the buyers.

In other words, when you see a Hammer, instead of thinking that this may signal a reversal (future tense), think of it as a sign that there has already been a change of direction (in the second half of the session), and now the question is whether this can be sustained, and whether it can turn into a solid change of direction for the market you're viewing.

Examples

Now I'm going to roll out one of my all time favourite charts; a weekly candlestick chart for the EUR/USD Forex cross, dating back to 1999. This was just a couple of years into the unified currency, when the euro was almost being classed as a laughing stock.

Source: CQG, Inc. © 2008 All rights reserved worldwide.

Figure 3-3: Euro vs. US Dollar Forex Cross; weekly candlestick chart; 29 May 2000 – 10 September 2001

So just to set the scene this is a weekly chart. The open of each candle is the first trade on the Forex markets on a Monday morning in Asia. The close is the last print on Friday night in the US.

As you can see, the market finished each big down-leg with a Hammer candlestick, which is all very nice, and suggests that these patterns are the best thing since sliced bread.

Except that's not why I've shown you this chart. I want you to take a closer look and find two more Hammers on the chart.

They appear halfway down the first move, both together, at the end of August 2000. The first week of September turned out to be one of the worst weeks for the euro on the whole chart. In other words our two Hammers didn't work. They were without doubt the worst possible signals of a reversal.

If you had a trading system based on buying the market on appearance of a Hammer on this chart, you would have been stopped out by the time the good signals came along. In fact you'd probably have abandoned the strategy altogether by then, if you had any money left!

One lesson we can learn from this is that we should never have a decision-making process based purely on one candlestick pattern being posted. This is common sense, surely. When you buy a jumper do you have one criterion, ie, "it must be red", and do you go out and buy the first red jumper you see? Or do you also want to have a certain type of neck, and a specific style, and a particular material or texture? Of course you do!

This is where academics get it all wrong where technical analysis is concerned. To put it in simple terms they look at something like candlestick analysis and say "we tested 500 occurrences of a Hammer and only 100 gave us a 300 point rally after they appeared, therefore candlesticks are rubbish." Thanks for nothing. Academics don't generally wear very nice jumpers, do they? Whereas technical analysts, in the main, are a well dressed bunch (myself apart!).

Look at Figure 3.4. Candlesticks B, C, D and G all qualify as Hammers.

B and C are the failed patterns that I've talked about above, but it's pretty clear to see that patterns D and G did a good job in calling a reversal. Or did they?

If you had used the filter of needing a green candle straight after a Hammer to give you a buy signal you would have refrained from taking buy signals at B and C, which would have turned out to be very good decisions. More to follow on this.

But you would have taken the signal after candlestick D at the end of the green candle straight after the Hammer, and then would have suffered three straight weeks of losses. In fact I'm pretty sure I would have stopped myself out at some point during those three weeks. I hope so anyway.

After Hammer G you would have waited for a green candle then bought, and made a tidy profit. No issues with this one at all.

Source: CQG, Inc. © 2008 All rights reserved worldwide.

Figure 3-4: Euro vs. US Dollar Forex Cross; weekly candlestick chart; 29 May 2000 – 10 September 2001 with annotations

So am I trying to say that this is great because it works 25% of the time? No, actually it worked 75% of the time in this case, if you had waited for a subsequent qualifying green candle.

Why 75%? Because many of the best traders in the world will tell you that saving money, and stopping yourself from making a bad trade, is as important as making money. If you read interviews with top traders, such as those in Jack Schwager's *Market Wizards*, you'll see repeated references to preservation of capital. This introduces something important to our usage of candlestick analysis that we haven't even considered yet: **candlesticks can be used to stay out of bad trades as well as to get you into good trades.**

Negative selection

Candlesticks can be used for negative selection. What does this mean? If you'd been watching this down-move with a view to waiting for an opportunity to get long, you would have saved yourself a lot of pain, misery and money by waiting for two criteria to be established: a bullish Hammer and a subsequent confirming candlestick. So you had a strategy to get you into good trades as well as keep you out of bad ones; to deselect or negatively select those that needed staying away from.

In the case of this chart we can take it a step further and redefine our criteria to give us better trade opportunities. We can say that if the market moves above the high from the Hammer week, then we will go long. With this filter we would still stay out of the market after candles B and C (a sigh of relief once again), get into the long trade much earlier after the Hammer D (nice), and get in slightly earlier after Candle G (still nice). Suddenly, just by applying a simple filter we have a powerful tool to help us spot not just when trends are changing, but also when they're not!

This introduces another factor to the equation: each chart will be different, and you should never treat any two charts the same. Yes, a Hammer is often a strong reversal pattern, but what you do with it can change from chart to chart.

This is in spite of the fact that one of the assumptions we make as technical analysts is that price action is repetitive; if something's happened many times before in a particular stock or security, we can assume it will probably happen in a similar way in the future. In the example above we worked out that looking for Hammers then waiting for a move through the Hammer's high would provide the most robust and timely signals over the life of this particular chart. We can now apply this set of rules to the same chart in future, making the assumption that market action is repetitive.

Obviously this isn't a guarantee that it will work out, but it stacks the odds in your favour. Backtesting is the name given to this exercise; going back in time to see what worked well before, so that you can apply this in the future. I often give seminars and talks where people gaze at me waiting to be given the Answer. Clearly if I had the Answer I'd be in the Bahamas on my yacht, keeping the Answer to myself. Unfortunately the answer to becoming a successful analyst or trader is hard work, which in this case involves the backtesting of patterns to see if they've done the job before.

In the following pages I've posted several examples of Hammers that have given us a low, or at least a good bounce. As you can see they don't all look exactly the same, and sometimes they don't actually appear right on the day the market bottoms out.

Source: CQG, Inc. © 2008 All rights reserved worldwide.

Figure 3-5: CBOT Dow futures (unadjusted active continuation); daily candlestick chart; 17 December 2004 – 16 February 2005, showing 28 January 2005 Hammer

Note how the Hammer pattern in Figure 3-5 didn't actually define the low of the move, but formed a secondary low that held the support level created by the low four days earlier.

Source: CQG, Inc. © 2008 All rights reserved worldwide.

Figure 3-6: CBOT Dow futures (unadjusted active continuation); daily candlestick chart; 25 June 2004 – 8 September 2004, showing 13 August 2004 Hammer

Another one where support was found at a support level from a few days earlier.

Source: CQG, Inc. © 2008 All rights reserved worldwide.

Figure 3-7: CBOT Dow futures (unadjusted active continuation); daily candlestick chart; 19 September 2000 – 8 November 2000, showing 18 October 2000 Hammer

A slightly odd looking example, but still a Hammer, and still a good reversal signal, as it turned out.

The colour of the real body on a Hammer

Finally, let's address a question that's often asked when it comes to this sort of single candlestick patterns: does it matter about the colour of the real body? No is the answer, and hopefully Figure 3-8 shows why it doesn't.

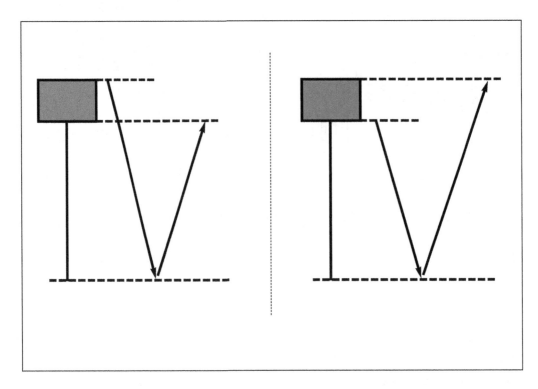

Figure 3-8: Red bodied and green bodied Hammers; any real difference in the message?

As you can see, in both cases the market sold off a long way, then came back a long way. Does it really matter in which order the open and close come? The fact is the bulls recovered from a pretty horrendous start to the day.

So no, the colour of the real body doesn't matter when it comes to the Hammer. Of course there may be a slight psychological edge ascribed to a green-bodied Hammer, as the trading at the end of the day managed to surpass the opening value, but in my experience the market makes very little differentiation between red and green real bodies on this pattern.

It's the length of the lower shadow that is probably more important, followed by what happens in the days after the Hammer is posted.

Hammer summary

A Hammer is a single candle reversal pattern that's found in a market that has been falling, with a small real body at the top end of the candle's range, which leaves a long lower shadow.

The Hammer is one of my favourite reversal patterns, whatever the time frame of the chart being viewed. I have found them to be particularly effective on liquid exchange-traded futures contracts like T-Notes, Bunds, the DAX Index and Gold, especially when viewing short-term time frames like 10-minute or 30-minute charts.

Later on when I expand upon different time frames we will see plenty more examples of Hammers. It really is an amazingly effective and powerful reversal pattern when used in the correct way!

More single candle patterns – Shooting Star, Hanging Man, Inverted Hammer

Having spent a good deal of time exploring the intricacies of the Hammer I hope you're now happy with the idea that a candlestick can be broken down into its component parts to work out the direction of travel that it represents. Armed with this we can now move on to several new patterns and quickly get a grasp of how they're formed and why they suggest a reversal.

The Hammer belongs to a family totalling 4 patterns, all with similar characteristics, ie, small real bodies at one extreme of the pattern, leaving one shadow much longer than the other.

The next such pattern that we'll dissect and study is the Shooting Star.

Shooting Star

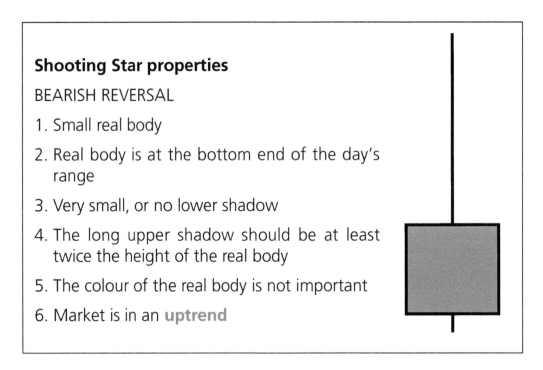

Shooting Star properties

BEARISH REVERSAL

1. Small real body

2. Real body is at the bottom end of the day's range

3. Very small, or no lower shadow

4. The long upper shadow should be at least twice the height of the real body

5. The colour of the real body is not important

6. Market is in an **uptrend**

Construction/getting inside the pattern

As you can see this is pretty much the opposite of the Hammer. This time the long upper shadow is at the top end of the day's range, and the real body is near the bottom. Also, we're looking for this pattern in a rising market as opposed to a downtrend.

So let's think about the price action that goes into the construction of a Shooting Star. Let's do the same thing as we did with the Hammer, and look at a live market example. Below is a daily candlestick chart for gold in May 2006 when highs not seen since the early 1980s were hit.

Source: CQG, Inc. © 2008 All rights reserved worldwide.

Figure 3-9: CBOT 100 oz Gold futures; daily (all sessions) candlestick continuation chart (no adjustment for roll-over); 10 April 2006 to 13 June 2006, showing Shooting Star Candlesticks on 12 May 2006 and 17 May 2006

As you can see there are actually two Shooting Star patterns on this chart, the one that defined the absolute top of the move, then another just 3 days later. The one we'll zoom in on is the first one, the high of the move. Let's look at a 15-minute chart for that day.

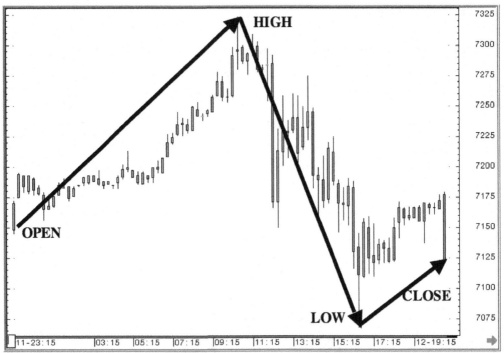

Source: CQG, Inc. © 2008 All rights reserved worldwide.

Figure 3-10: CBOT 100 oz Gold futures; 15-minute candlestick chart (all sessions); 12 May 2006

On the intra-day chart in Figure 3-10 we have plotted the four pieces of data that make up the Shooting Star on the daily candlestick chart: that day's open, high, low and close. As you can see, the direction of travel on the day was upwards in the early part of the session, followed by weakness in the second half, culminating in a weak close.

This is the opposite of the Hammer. Instead of a "V" shaped direction of travel we see an arc or "A" shaped movement.

The bulls are in charge going into the session, remember that. So when the maarket starts to rally in morning trade no one is surprised. The bulls continue on their happy way while the bears continue to get beaten up.

But at 732.3 the balance between buyers and sellers changes and the buyers are suddenly not dominating. The second half of the session, as evidenced by the wild assortment of candlesticks, was a ding-dong affair.

Psychology

I often talk about charts and the markets using sporting analogies, many of these using my beloved football, or soccer to those living anywhere other than the UK.

This session was akin to a match that was pretty quiet and predictable in the first half, and honours went to the team in green, who trotted in 1-0 up at half time. Incidentally the team in green had won 5 of their last 6 matches, so no one was that surprised that they were winning this one, especially as the reds were near the bottom of the league.

But in football sometimes things change. Manchester United aren't going to be the best team in the land forever, thank heavens!

The red team's manager says something at half-time, and the second half starts with a bang. Over the next 45 minutes we are treated to the best display of football in living memory, with goals galore, and by the end of the game the reds win 5-4.

Whose fans go home happier? Which team is likely to feel better going into the next game? Generally the team that dominates the second half of a match will finish the stronger and win the match. It is exactly the same with a day in the life of the markets. If the bulls win the first half, but the bears win the second half, and the bears keep their pressure on until the end, we'll likely post a candlestick with a long upper shadow; often a Shooting Star.

Can you see how even a single candlestick can be an extremely effective reader of price action over a particular time period?

I may seem like a stuck record at the moment, but by making sure you get used to the idea of thinking about the direction of travel that goes into the construction of a particular shaped candlestick, you will breeze through the rest of this book, and candlesticks will immediately become a strong ally in your trading or reading of the markets.

Examples

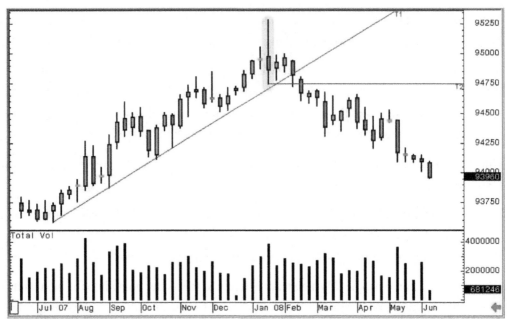

Source: CQG, Inc. © 2008 All rights reserved worldwide.

Figure 3-11: LIFFE June 2008 Short Sterling futures; weekly candlestick chart; 18 June 2007 – 9 June 2008

You can see from the chart that the top of this move was defined by a Shooting Star in the week of 21 January 2008 – 25 January 2008. Although there is a bit of lower shadow showing on this candle I'm sure you'll agree that the long upper shadow definitely smacked of a rejection of the upside. Another reason I like this chart is because of the two previous examples in mid-November and late November. Again neither was a textbook example, and in these instances they didn't lead to a reversal. The big jump in volume, and the sheer volatility of the candlestick that actually gave us the top, alerted us that it was something not to be ignored. The break of trend support (labelled T1 on the chart) a few weeks later confirmed our suspicions, and the subsequent break of the bottom of the Shooting Star week (the horizontal line labelled T2) added further weight to the argument for a top.

Source: CQG, Inc. © 2008 All rights reserved worldwide.

Figure 3-12: LIFFE June 2008 Short Sterling futures; 60-minute candlestick chart; 21 January 2008 – 25 January 2008

This is a short-term chart showing direction of travel over the course of the Shooting Star week highlighted in Figure 3-11.

Another example

Source: CQG, Inc. © 2008 All rights reserved worldwide.

Figure 3-13: Eurex September 2008 Bund futures; 30-minute candlestick chart; 6 and 9 June 2008

The move in the first few hours of this particular morning came as something of a surprise at the time, but the market was in a downtrend overall, so many traders were looking for a chance to sell any strength. The up move ended with a high volume Shooting Star on the 30-minute candle chart. A severe sell off followed.

The colour of the real body

As with the Hammer we are relatively unconcerned by the colour of the real body for a Shooting Star, although a red real body does show that the market sold off through the opening price towards the end of the candle's life, and therefore it may carry slightly more significance. It's not essential for the pattern though, and Shooting Stars are generally credited with being a powerful reversal pattern, whatever the colour of the real body.

Shooting Star summary

You can see that the Shooting Star is the exact opposite to the Hammer. The construction and psychology are exactly the same but in reverse.

It is a single candlestick in a rising market with a long upper shadow and a small real body at the bottom end of the candle's range.

In summing up the Hammer I said that it was one of my favourites, so it follows that its bearish opposite number will also be high on my list. It is indeed. These patterns are so simple yet so effective. Just the sort of technical analysis I like!

As with the Hammer it's also worth highlighting that these are generally great patterns to look out for on short-term charts (10 to 30-minute) for futures contracts or equities that trade with a combination of good volume and volatility.

Now we're going to look at two familiar looking patterns, and work out why they are given different names to those we've come across already.

Inverted Hammer

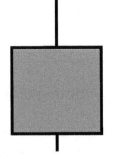

Inverted Hammer properties

BULLISH REVERSAL

1. Small real body

2. Real body is at the bottom end of the day's range

3. Very small, or no lower shadow

4. The long upper shadow should be at least twice the height of the real body

5. The colour of the real body is not important

6. Market is in a **downtrend**

Getting inside the pattern

Does this shape of candlestick look familiar? It should do, because it's exactly the same shape as a Shooting Star, in fact conditions 1, 2, 3, 4, and 5 are all the same. The only difference is the last condition, ie, what the trend is when we see a pattern of this shape.

If you see a candlestick shaped like a Shooting Star during a downtrending market, you're looking at an Inverted Hammer, which is a bullish reversal pattern.

It's not the strongest of patterns, and if we once again go through the steps of thinking about the price action, we'll soon see why. We are in a downtrending market, so the bears are dominating. On this day we see a strong rally followed by a sell-off, which gives us the long upper shadow. As with the Shooting Star the market moves in an arc shaped direction of travel, moving higher then lower.

So why could this possibly be a reversal? After all, by the end of the day we're back on the lows and the bears are dominating.

Psychology

Well, here's the thing. The bulls did give us that move higher in the early part of the session, so they can make a difference. They showed an ability to move the market higher, even if on this particular occasion they couldn't sustain the push to the upside. The selling in the second half of the day saw the market move back down to where it started, more or less.

So possibly this is more of a warning signal, rather than a strong reversal signal *per se*.

In my experience these do not make strong reversal patterns, but can appear in the run up to a bottom, so can serve a purpose in warning us that things may be changing.

But don't take my word for it: if you have a favoured market that you trade, and a favoured time frame for your trading, you should fire up a chart that suits your needs and look back to find the candlestick patterns that have done a good job historically. We can make the assumption that the participants in the market you're viewing don't change dramatically over time, so patterns of behaviour can and will be repeated, and the candlestick chart is merely a representation of the behaviour of the market in any instrument. So if Inverted Hammers work beautifully on your chart, then place more importance on the next one you see.

This is why I shy away from giving candlestick reversal patterns a star rating on their potency: it's because some patterns work better in certain markets than others, and the only way to decide what provides the strongest signal is to do the leg-work and backtest to find what worked best in the past **for your market on your chart.**

A note about backtesting

Backtesting involves going back over historical data on your chart, whatever the time frame, to test a trading strategy. It is a useful (arguably essential) exercise, except that most people aren't honest with themselves about the reality of their entries or exits.

I always suggest a "worst case scenario" approach to this. Say for example you get a buy signal after a candle with a close at 1.10, and the next candle sees the market trade up from an open at 1.12 to a close at 1.20. Do you say you bought at 1.10, 1.12 or 1.20?

My answer would be 1.20, because in reality you wouldn't pay 1.10 because you don't know until after the close on that first day that you've got a buy signal. You may pay 1.12, as you would attempt to enter the market early on the second day, but what happens if the market traded a tiny amount at 1.12 then immediately jumped to 1.20? Here is a fact: unless you have access to the intra-day data you would be making baseless and dangerous assumptions about where you entered the trade.

Why not work on a "worst case scenario" and if your trading strategy still makes money, then it should do even better when the slippage is taken out. One more thing to think about regarding backtesting: you have to pay your broker's commission, or your trading fees, so this also needs to be in the equation. I've seen so many trading systems presented where the results exclude commission costs. I would like their broker's name, as I too would like to trade with zero commission!

Finally, you also might want to add a little word called reality into the equation when you're backtesting strategies. For example once a month, on the first Friday, we get the US Employment Report, and the world's debt markets go berserk. Are you happy to take a signal from your system two minutes before this regularly market-moving event? A release that you know could move the market significantly up or down? Or would you want to put on a trade hours before a big interest rate announcement, or a company's results, or a crop report? Some would say yes, and I'm not going to argue with them. We all have our own different risk parameters. All I'm pointing out is that **if** you are uncomfortable with this sort of trading then you can't include these pre-event signals in your test results, even if most of the trades worked well. If in reality you'd never have put the trades on, then you're kidding yourself!

Examples

Source: CQG, Inc. © 2008 All rights reserved worldwide.

Figure 3-14: HSBC plc; daily candlestick chart; 31 January 2007 – 11 May 2007, showing 28 February 2007 Inverted Hammer

This Inverted Hammer didn't signal an end to the trend, but if you had allowed yourself to consider the idea of a reversal after you'd seen it, you wouldn't have been so surprised when the market bottomed out a few weeks later.

The bottom, as you can see, was a Hammer day with a lower shadow that had breached the previous support. Even then, there were a few more small bodied candlesticks seen after that before the bulls finally got their act together.

The following chart is interesting, as it has a plethora of Inverted Hammers, as highlighted. This once again proves the importance of confirmation for any candlestick pattern. If your trading strategy in this instance was "if we see an Inverted Hammer then buy" you wouldn't have any money left after the first three to take advantage of the fourth pattern, the one that did actually give us a reversal.

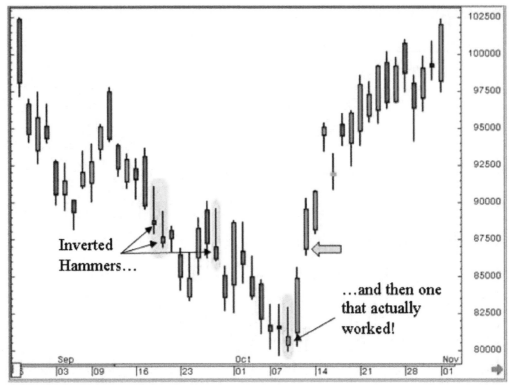

Source: CQG, Inc. © 2008 All rights reserved worldwide.

Figure 3-15: CME NASDAQ futures (unadjusted active continuation); daily candlestick chart; 27 August 2002 – 1 November 2002, showing Inverted Hammers on 18 September, 19 September, 27 September and 9 October

But if you'd simply asked to see a green candlestick following the Inverted Hammer you would have stayed out of the first three and jumped in after the fourth one, when the market gapped higher two days later (as highlighted by the light blue arrow). Even though you would be buying 68 ticks off the lows, you still wouldn't be complaining. Also you could have placed your initial stop below gap support at 856. Nice. Incidentally this was the absolute low of this index after the dotcom bubble had burst.

Inverted Hammer summary

Inverted Hammer summary

The Inverted Hammer isn't generally the strongest of reversal patterns. However, it can be a good warning of an impending reversal because it's a candle that illustrates that the bulls aren't completely dead and buried; they're starting to make noises, even if on this occasion it came to nothing because the bears stepped back in to sell into the gains towards the end of the formation of the candle.

One reason I wanted to cover this pattern was to complete the picture and differentiate it from the similarly shaped Shooting Star.

Hanging Man

The last candlestick in this family is the Hanging Man, and what a marvellously descriptive name it has! Does anyone think this might be a bullish pattern? No, I didn't think so! There can't be much upside to being strung up on the gallows, I've always felt.

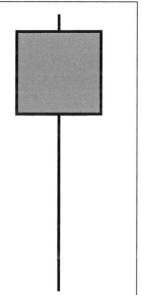

Hanging Man properties

BEARISH REVERSAL

1. Small real body

2. Real body is at the top end of the day's range

3. Very small, or no upper shadow

4. The long lower shadow should be at least twice the height of the real body

5. The colour of the real body is not important

6. Market is in an **uptrend**

Getting inside the pattern

We've established, just by hearing the name, that this is a bearish pattern. As we can see from the properties panel it's the same shape as the Hammer, except this time it's seen during a rising market. Our first five rules are exactly the same, it's just the last one, the "where" rule, that changes.

A Hanging Man is formed during an uptrend on a day when the market sells off then rallies to take back most or all of the losses seen earlier in the session. It represents a "V" shaped direction of travel over the course of the life of the candle.

As with the Inverted Hammer the idea of this being a reversal is a little tough to grasp at first as we're talking about a candlestick that's formed by a market that sold off early on, but was rising neatly again by the time the session ended.

Psychology

The reasoning behind this pattern is akin to the Inverted Hammer, but in reverse: the long lower shadow shows that the bears managed to push things lower, even if they couldn't sustain the push over the course of the whole day. The point is they gave it a go, so they're not completely dead in the water. It's possible they're waking up and may in the near future be capable of mounting something a little more sustainable.

Examples

Source: CQG, Inc. © 2008 All rights reserved worldwide.

Figure 3-16: ICE Brent Crude Oil futures (unadjusted active continuation); daily candlestick chart; 27 December 2005 – 15 February 2006, showing Hanging Man on 30 January 2006

On this chart a Hanging Man sandwiched in between two similar highs was posted. Once the low between these highs was broken a Western chart pattern called a Double Top had been completed. The Hanging Man wasn't really the main driver of any change of trend at this time, however it would have added a bit of weight to one's conviction once the sell signal given by the Double Top was seen a few days later.

Source: CQG, Inc. © 2008 All rights reserved worldwide.

Figure 3-17: Euro vs US Dollar Forex Cross; weekly candlestick chart; 29 May 2000 – 10 September 2001 with annotations

We've seen this chart already: we used it when we were looking at the Hammer pattern (Figure 3-4). We came to the conclusion that Candles B, C, D and G were the Hammers, and that the others didn't qualify.

We can now embellish on this and say that E and F qualify as Hanging Man candlesticks, as they're both Hammer-shaped, but seen in a rising market. We can also safely say that while Hanging Man candlesticks don't generally provide strong signals, in this case they did.

What about A and H? Argue amongst yourselves! If anything they're Hanging Man candles, as they're seen just off the highs.

Hanging Man summary

A Hanging Man candlestick is the same shape as a Hammer, but is seen during a rising market.

I'm sure you'll agree with me that after finding out all about this pattern it's a bit of an anticlimax. What a great name, summoning up the most bearish of bear thoughts! In reality it can be a good warning signal that the sellers are stirring after a period of domination by the bulls, but it's not often the horrid disaster that its name might suggest!

Different types of Doji – Gravestones, Dragonflies, and the Rickshaw Man

We've had a look at Doji candlesticks already, but there are a few hybrid Doji candles, and now is a good time to look at these, as they are also variations on the patterns we've covered above.

A candlestick is described as a Doji wherever the open and close are, as long as they're close to each other. We may open and close near the bottom, near the middle, or near the top of a day's range. As long as there is a small real body, it qualifies as a Doji. So let's look at three entirely different Doji candlesticks, just to prove the point.

Gravestone Doji

Rules

Gravestone Doji properties

BEARISH REVERSAL

1. No (or a VERY small) real body

2. The open and close are at or very close to the bottom of the candle, leaving no lower shadow

3. A long upper shadow

4. Market is in an **uptrend**

Once again the first of these patterns has been named rather aptly. Let's face it, there's little doubt that a Gravestone Doji must be a bearish pattern. So what is a Gravestone Doji? It's a Doji seen in an uptrending market, with an open and close at the bottom of the day's range.

Getting inside the pattern

Let's briefly step through the price action that goes into this one. We rally right from the very first trade, but at some point the buying runs out of steam and the market starts to sell off. This selling sees us right back down to the first trade of the day and the market closed at this level, leaving absolutely no (or a very small) lower shadow, as well as no (or a very small) real body.

Psychology

The buyers dominated early on, but it was all in vain, and the market was back on the day's low by the time the bell went to send us all home.

What does this description sound like? Exactly like a Shooting Star, I hope you're thinking to yourself.

It's the ultimate Shooting Star, if you like, because the market closed on the day's low, but also because the powerful Doji is combined with the powerful Shooting Star: a double whammy power play. It has an "A" shaped direction of travel with a close on the low.

Examples

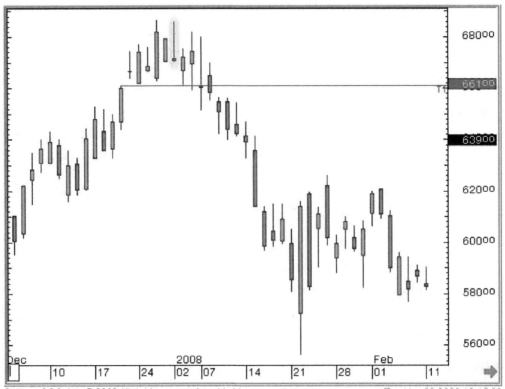

Source: CQG, Inc. © 2008 All rights reserved worldwide.

Figure 3-18: Reed Elsevier; daily candlestick chart; 4 December 2007 – 11 February 2008, showing Gravestone Doji on 2 January

At the time that this Gravestone Doji was posted there was a gap support below at 661, but once this broke on a closing basis on 8 January the selling started in earnest.

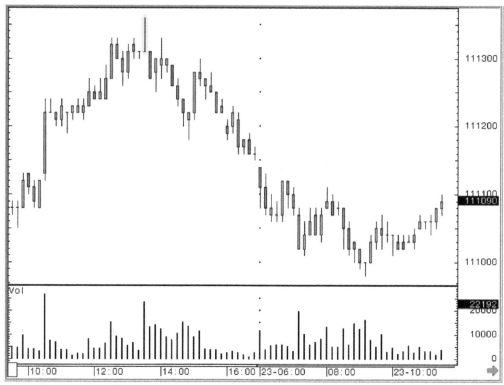

Source: CQG, Inc. © 2008 All rights reserved worldwide.

Figure 3-19: Eurex Bobl futures; 10-minute candlestick chart; 22 & 23 April 2003

Figure 3-19 is a 10-minute chart for the Bobl futures, so each candlestick represents a mere 10 minutes' worth of trade. As you can see the Gravestone Doji was posted around lunchtime on 22 April, making a new high for the day in the process with a 111.36 print. The market then headed steadily south from this moment onwards for the rest of the day, closing at 111.16. We will revisit this chart a little later as there's a lot more to say on it.

> ### Gravestone Doji summary
>
> A Gravestone Doji is the ultimate Shooting Star; a Doji candlestick, with an open and close at very similar levels, in this instance right on or very near the candle's low.
>
> This pattern is indeed something to feel rather morbid about, especially if you've been riding a strong uptrend. Your time might be up...

Dragonfly Doji

Rules

Dragonfly Doji properties

BULLISH REVERSAL

1. No (or a VERY small) real body
2. The open and close are at or very close to the top of the candle, leaving no upper shadow
3. A long lower shadow
4. Market is in a **downtrend**

Getting inside the pattern

What we have here is a Doji in a downtrending market with an open and close at the top end of the day's range. This means the market sold off from the first trade, then recovered these losses to end the session right back where it started.

Psychology

The bears were winning the accolades early on but at some point (at the low to be precise) this balance of power changed, and from this point onwards the bulls dominated, right up until the close, which was also the high of the day and right back where the market started.

This has a similar psychology to the Hammer in that the market had a shocking start to proceedings, but had recovered nicely by the time the session finished, which could empower the bulls going forward.

This kind of pattern has two names that I've come across: a Dragonfly Doji, or an Umbrella Doji. Both are fairly descriptive of the shape, and obviously we're talking about a bullish pattern if seen in a downward trend.

As with the Gravestone Doji, the fact that we're talking about a Doji that also has all the attributes of a Hammer means it is a pattern that's generally very powerful.

Example

Have a look at the chart in Figure 3-20. It's the same chart as I showed earlier, with the Gravestone Doji on the high, except this time we're looking at the developing downtrend, and we note that this ended a few hours into 23 April with a Dragonfly/Umbrella Doji.

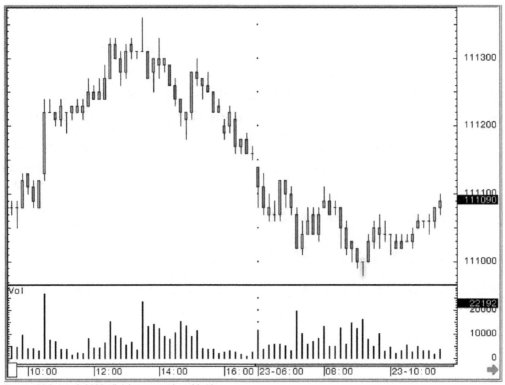

Source: CQG, Inc. © 2008 All rights reserved worldwide.

Figure 3-20: Eurex Bobl futures; 10-minute candlestick chart; 22 & 23 April 2003

You may be wondering why I'm using an intra-day chart from 2003. Do these patterns turn up so rarely? It's not so much that. I class this chart as one of my old favourites. It has featured in my seminars for many years, and for good reason.

And we haven't finished with it just yet. We will come back to it for a third time in the next section, where we discuss the importance of volume to confirm candlestick patterns.

Dragonfly Doji summary

A Dragonfly Doji or Umbrella Doji is generally a strong reversal pattern in a downtrending market. It is a Doji with an open and close at the top of the candlestick, leaving the real body looking like a line across the top of a vertical line, hence the rather descriptive names. These Doji look like an Umbrella or a Dragonfly. Not a pattern to be ignored.

Rickshaw Man

Rickshaw Man properties

REVERSAL

1. No (or a VERY small) real body

2. The open and close are at or very close to the middle of the candle

3. This means the upper and lower shadows are equal in length

4. A reversal pattern in an **uptrend** or a **downtrend**

Inside the pattern

The final pattern of this triumvirate is the marvellously named Rickshaw Man. This is a Doji with an open and close at, or very close to, the middle of the candle's range.

Psychology

An open and close bang in the middle of the candle's range, then. The failed attempt higher had equal price attributes to the selling to the lows that also proved to be unsuccessful. This can be classed as the ultimate in indecision. There was an almost total balance between buyers and sellers. Obviously if you see this sort of thing at an extreme high or an extreme low there may be a change afoot.

Examples

Source: CQG, Inc. © 2008 All rights reserved worldwide.

Figure 3-21: CBOT Corn futures (Pit session, unadjusted continuation chart); weekly candlestick chart; 13 October 2003 – 23 August 2004, showing Rickshaw Man on week of 5 – 9 April 2004

This near perfect Rickshaw Man right at the top of a move in corn gave us a significant top.

If you missed shorting this, the Shooting Star a couple of months later gave you another signal that the market was toppy.

Source: CQG, Inc. © 2008 All rights reserved worldwide.

Figure 3-22: Eurex Bobl futures; daily candlestick chart (adjusted continuation); 11 February 2008 – 23 April 2008, showing 17 March Rickshaw Man

The Rickshaw Man at the top of this chart signalled a high in the Bobl in March 2008. Hopefully you've noticed that this pattern was seen while the market was testing an important resistance – the high from a few days earlier. Four days later the market completed a Double Top and the significant sell signal we got from this combination served the bears well.

Rickshaw Man summary

A Rickshaw Man is a Doji with an open and close near the middle of the candle's range. I have to admit it took a while to find really good examples of this pattern, which proves that maybe it is only in here because its name has mildly amusing connotations of confused men carting Rickshaws around, unable to work out which direction to take next! I wouldn't devote too much time in the pursuit of the perfect Rickshaw Man; there are better ways to spend your time!

The importance of volume for confirming candlesticks and why candlesticks work whatever the market, whatever the time frame

Looking at these Doji patterns is a good time to introduce an important aspect of any reading of candlestick charts: volume.

What does "volume" mean?

Volume is, quite simply, the amount of trade going through at each price or each period of time. If volume is light you can assume that the price action you're seeing may not be the real deal.

If you see a move on strong volume you can be assured that the move is the result of strong buying or selling, and therefore there's some sustainability to the move in question. Quite simply, accompanying volume is one of the best ways to confirm any candlestick pattern, but if you see a reversal pattern (or a major price move) on very weak volume you should treat it as suspect.

Volume is illustrated on a candlestick chart in a separate box below the main body of the chart, usually expressed as a histogram. There have been attempts to incorporate volume into the candlesticks themselves. One example is an Equivolume candle chart, where the width of the real body varies depending on whether it was accompanied by strong or weak volume. The fatter the body the more volume was seen. I've never been that much of a fan, but that's possibly because I started off with bar charts, and I got used to having volume down at the bottom below the prices.

Coming from a trading floor background I always felt that volume was a great word to describe trading activity. If you were in the coffee lounge behind the LIFFE Floor, you could hear a change in noise level from the market, and even if you didn't you soon heard the noise of feet running back to the floor because something had happened to cause a sudden leap in activity.

Even today in a dealing room at one of the large banks or brokers you can tell almost instantly whether a market is quiet or busy. I think this is where a lot of remote traders miss out when they sit and trade from home. They can try to re-create this by using the business news channels or a Squawk service for "ambient" noise, but the best tool the chartist has for tracking activity is the volume histogram.

A jump in volume means something's happening. A candlestick pattern that's got (relatively) large volume accompanying it generally makes for a stronger signal.

Example

Let's go back to our old favourite chart from the end of the last section to illustrate this point:

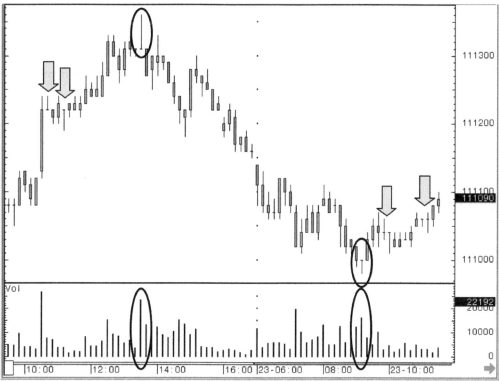

Source: CQG, Inc. © 2008 All rights reserved worldwide.

Figure 3-23: Eurex Bobl futures; 10-minute candlestick chart; 22 & 23 April 2003

You can see that both the candlesticks I highlighted, the Gravestone Doji and the Dragonfly Doji, were particularly strong in the volume department. I have also highlighted a few other Doji candlesticks on this chart (with the blue down arrows), but as you can see if you look down to the volume histogram, there was no significant accompanying activity; this suggests that these Doji were probably the result of indifference rather than a big two way swing between buyers and sellers that could have trend changing significance.

Note regarding Doji on short-term charts

I purposely chose Doji to illustrate the point about volume, because when markets get quiet you get a lot of Doji. This is quite simply because volatility is very low, and therefore the chances of opening and closing at the same levels increases.

I spend a lot of time looking at short time frame charts, but find that candlesticks work well whatever the time frame, something that this chart once again illustrates very well.

The Doji candles that were formed on light volume were merely the result of the market going sideways; marking time because no one was actually around to trade. They appear over lunchtime when the morning rush is done and the market is waiting for the US session to get underway. They're often the result of half the market going out to buy a sandwich, rather than any major reversal in thinking about the market.

A closer look at our Dragonfly Doji example

If you took a look at our Dragonfly Doji in Figure 3-23 without the assistance of the volume histogram you'd surely class it as a similar deal, based on it being such a tight range. In this 10-minute period only three different prices were traded, 111.00, 110.99 and 110.98. The market opened and closed at 111.00, hence there is no real body, just a line at the top of the candle. If we add the volume into the equation we suddenly realise that this 10-minute period with an extremely tight range was actually one of the busiest 10-minute periods over the whole day. Neither the bulls nor the bears appeared to have achieved much, but they certainly had a good old go at each other, and because the market was on the day's lows, and had sold off 38 ticks from the high of the previous afternoon, the bulls can be rightfully happy with their work. In fact you could almost argue that there was someone out there who wasn't prepared to see the market drop below the psychologically important 111.00 mark, and spent that entire 10-minute period hoovering up the sell orders and making sure the market was always bid over, so that the sellers eventually realised they'd hit a brick wall.

Psychology

Generally if you hit a brick wall there's only one way to go, and it's no exception in the markets. The sellers walked away after our high volume tiddler of a Dragonfly Doji, but it was only the volume that highlighted how significant this candlestick actually was. Without the volume we wouldn't have realised the significance of this Doji.

More on the subject of short-term trading

A question I often get asked is whether candlesticks work well in time frames other than the daily chart, particularly for short-term traders. My answer is a categorical "Yes." In my daily analysis I view 10-minute, 60-minute and daily candlestick charts all the time, and during the course of a day constantly spot reversal patterns on the 10-minute chart. The nice thing about this is the instant gratification that they can provide. While on a daily chart you have to wait 2 days to see a Hammer and a green candle to confirm it, on a 10-minute chart this would only take 20 minutes. The message is exactly the same: the Hammer is a period of time where the market sells off then rallies to retake the earlier losses. The green candle adds its weight to the argument for a reversal. It doesn't matter whether this combination of movements takes two days or 20 minutes, the market still need to do exactly that to get those two candles. I will spend a bit more time on these ideas later on (see pages 125-126).

With these patterns you should always look for confirming volume, which proves that a battle has indeed taken place at this time.

In fact on short-term time frames candlesticks like Shooting Stars and Hammers make even more sense. If you've ever spent any amount of time looking at a day session unfolding you'll see times when stops are triggered and the market heads quickly off in one direction, especially when an old support or resistance level is breached, only for the move to suddenly reverse. To use a Hammer as an example, the big traders look for places where small, weaker traders have their sell stops, and they trigger these stops, then flip their direction and start buying the market, taking it back through the old support level as quickly as the stops had seen us drop below there. This sort of price behaviour generally leaves a long lower shadow on the short-term charts, or a Hammer to you or me.

Chapter summary

Having read this chapter you should now be aware of those key candlestick patterns that are constructed of just one candlestick.

- The Hammer and Shooting Star are strong reversal patterns whatever the time frame viewed.

- The Hanging Man and the Inverted Hammer may be similar in shape to the Hammer and the Shooting Star, but they're seen in different trends, and as such their impact is usually greatly reduced.

- Doji are powerful reversal patterns in downtrends and uptrends, and are very easy to spot due to the lack of real body.

- Volume is another important element to consider when viewing candlestick charts.

We will now move on to reversal patterns that are constructed using more than one candlestick.

4

Multiple Reversal Patterns

The last chapter walked us through the commonly used single candlestick patterns, and hopefully by now you can look at any candlestick and be able to work out what sequence of events led to its formation as far as the combination of open, high, low and close is concerned.

We will now take things further by looking at combinations of candlesticks that make patterns that are made up of more than one candlestick.

Once again it's all about the direction of travel that has to occur to form a particular shape or colour of candlestick, and once again it should pretty much make sense if you take this approach. Do you remember how a Shooting Star is formed by an arc shaped direction of travel – gains then weakness? Well, most of the bearish reversal patterns discussed in this chapter do exactly this, except that the movement occurs over several candlesticks as opposed to just one.

I have deliberately made this chapter a little less structured than the material we've already covered, as you should now be well versed in the idea that candles are formed by a certain sequence of events, and that assumptions can be made from that.

I have retained the rules section and the summary for quick and easy reference.

Engulfing patterns

In my experience one of the most potent set of reversal patterns.

Bearish Engulfing Pattern

Bearish Engulfing Pattern properties

BEARISH REVERSAL

1. Two candle pattern

2. The first candle has an open real body, in line with the Bull trend

3. The second candle has a filled real body

4. The second candle's real body surrounds the real body of the first

5. The size and position of the shadows on either candles does not matter

6. The market is in an **uptrend** when the pattern appears

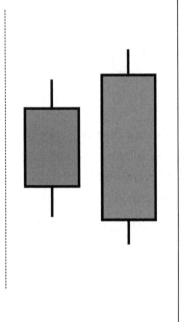

Let's think about the two sessions that make up our pattern. On day one the market goes up, as evidenced by the open bodied candlestick. The market is in an uptrend, so this is no surprise, and by the end of this session all's well in the world if you're bullish.

On the second session the market opened stronger, above the previous day's close, so once again things are going well if you're long. But then it all changes; the sellers are resurgent, and by the end of this session the market has sold off. The filled real body that surrounds or engulfs the open real body preceding it means enough has been sold off to give back all of the gains made the day before, and a bit more. From the first day's open to the second day's close the market is lower, having been a lot higher in between times.

So there is an arc shaped direction of travel, a rise then a drop, and a weak close to boot.

But there's more to it than that, because quite often a Bearish Engulfing Pattern starts off with a dramatically stronger open, like that illustrated in Figure 4-1, and this means there are several big "lines in the sand" to the immediate downside, which could and should act as support if the bulls are on their game.

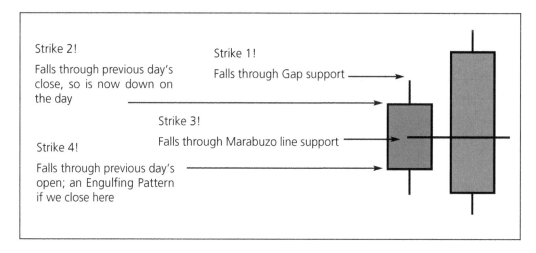

Figure 4-1: The four stages of a Bearish Engulfing Pattern

Let's go through this one stage at a time. On the second day, if the market opens above the previous day's high, there is a gap. The bulls often step in and buy weakness to the gap, but on this occasion the market falls through the gap support. Strike 1 to the beaten up bears.

There is then some selling off through the previous day's close. Strike 2. This, in turn, is followed by a sell off through the Marabuzo line (see page 81) of the green candle – Strike 3. This will further encourage the bears, who by now are starting to realise they're having a rare good day!

To post a Bearish Engulfing Pattern though, you need to surround the real body of the preceding candle, so the previous day's open is another important line in the sand. Strike 4! That's a fair bit of work for the bears to get through in one day, especially when you consider that we're in an uptrend, and they haven't been achieving much lately. The final thing, of course, is that the market has to close low as well (below the first day's open) for it to qualify as an Engulfing Pattern, so the selling has to be sustained into the close.

Engulfing patterns versus outside days

There is a pattern in Western analysis called a bearish outside day, or a key reversal day. The rule set for this is a bear day in a rising market with a high above the previous day's high and a low below the previous day's low. In other words the day's range is outside that of the day before, and a weak close is posted. This is pretty similar to an Engulfing Pattern, but not always, as the candlestick version doesn't necessarily require a greater range on day two, just a larger (filled) real body. In other words the range doesn't have to come into the equation.

Examples

Source: CQG, Inc. © 2008 All rights reserved worldwide.

Figure 4-2: AMEC plc; daily candlestick chart; 16 October 2007 – 24 January 2008, showing Bearish Engulfing Pattern on 3 and 4 January

On the 4 January a key support level was also broken at 820, and the move through here produced a Western Double Top formation as the market broke down through the low from a few sessions previous (24 December 2007). The other thing to note about this chart is how the market failed right on the resistance from a few months before.

Source: CQG, Inc. © 2008 All rights reserved worldwide.

Figure 4-3: ICE Brent Crude Oil futures (all sessions, active unadjusted continuation); daily candlestick chart; 30 November 2007 – 11 February 2008, showing 3 and 4 January 2008 Bearish Engulfing Pattern

This Bearish Engulfing Pattern saw a red candle surrounding a Star (see page 9) made the day before. We'd made a new all time high on the first candle of our pattern. Immediately after the Bearish Engulfing Pattern another big red candle was posted, so there was some instant gratification. There was an uptrend line to break before we got too excited though, and you can see there was another solid reaction to the downside once this line gave way. This is an important point to make: even if you had seen the reversal pattern, but then waited for the trend line to break, you still could have made good money on the down move, even if you only started selling $5 off the highs.

My particular favourites are combination patterns where we see something like a Shooting Star that is then engulfed by the next candlestick; the engulfing line adds weight to the initial signal. As always, though, we'd look for confirmation after the event before we'd act.

The ideal world volume characteristics of this pattern is higher volume on the second candlestick, ie, the selling on the second day is more ferocious than the buying that was seen on the first.

Bearish Engulfing Pattern summary

The Bearish Engulfing Pattern is a two candle pattern in a rising market where the second candle has a filled real body that surrounds the open real body before it. This is generally a strong reversal pattern as it often takes a lot of effort and achievement from the bears for it to form. It is one of my particular favourites for this reason. Also it usually coincides with the Western bearish outside day. It should be ignored at your peril!

Bullish Engulfing Pattern

Bullish Engulfing Pattern properties

BULLISH REVERSAL

1. Two candle pattern

2. The first candle has a filled real body, in line with the Bear trend

3. The second candle has an open real body

4. The second candle's real body surrounds the real body of the first

5. The position of the shadows on either candles does not matter

6. The market is in a downtrend when the pattern appears

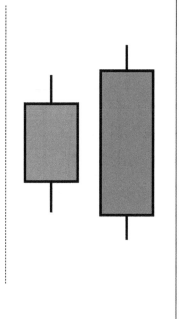

The opposite of a Bearish Engulfing Pattern is, as you might guess, a Bullish Engulfing Pattern. It is similarly powerful, and the set of rules is the same but in reverse.

The Bullish Engulfing Pattern suggests that a market has found support, and depicts two sessions where the bears dominate the first day but the bulls come back to life in some style in the second session.

It's the same sort of price action as can be seen during a Hammer candlestick, except it happens over two sessions.

Once again, all you have to do is think about the price action that goes into the separate candlesticks, and immediately you can see why it's a potential reversal. The second candle is akin to the second half of a Hammer session; the bulls suddenly wake up, and come storming back to the party. The market has to close strongly as well for it to engulf the first candle's real body. All of this bullishness comes after a weak open on the second day, so it's quite a revival that's been achieved.

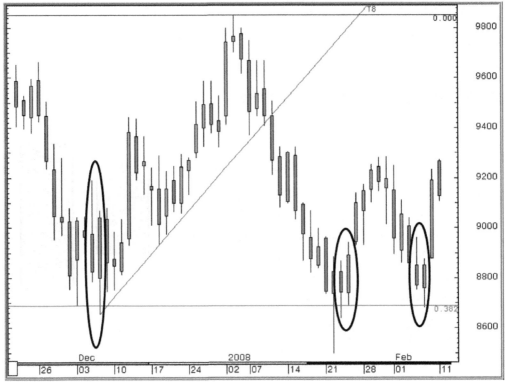

Source: CQG, Inc. © 2008 All rights reserved worldwide.

Figure 4-4: ICE Brent Crude Oil futures (all sessions, active unadjusted continuation); daily candlestick chart; 21 November 2007 – 11 February 2008, showing Bullish Engulfing Patterns on 5/6 December 2007, 23/24 January 2008, and 6/7 February 2008

This chart shows three Bullish Engulfing Patterns after pullbacks in Brent Crude at the end of 2007 and the beginning of 2008. If you look at a much longer-term chart for this one you'll see that the market was up near (what was then) all time highs having rallied strongly in the previous couple of years. The preceding chart merely shows some short-term pullbacks near the top of this bigger picture move.

Important note

We were in a long-term uptrend, there's no doubt about that. In fact the trend was so strong that there would be many people out there looking for a buying opportunity, either because they've missed making money on the previous up-leg, or because they've covered longs and are now looking to get long once more on any weakness.

On these three occasions the market pulled back to a short-term Fibonacci retracement level, then the Bullish Engulfing Patterns appeared.

Bullish Engulfing Pattern summary

The Bullish Engulfing Pattern is two candles; the first a filled candle in a downtrend. The change occurs on the second candle when the bulls have a great day after a bad start, and they manage to post a close on day two above the open on day one.

This is generally a strong reversal pattern, and one I'd recommend keeping an eye out for.

The next pair of patterns we're going to look at is Dark Cloud Cover and the Piercing Pattern.

Dark Cloud Cover

Dark Cloud Cover properties

BEARISH REVERSAL

1. Two candle pattern

2. The first candle has an open real body, in line with the Bull trend

3. The market gaps higher on the open of the second candle

4. The second candle has a filled real body

5. The second candle's body closes 'well into' the body of the first, ie, below the halfway mark of the first candle's real body

6. The market is in an **uptrend**

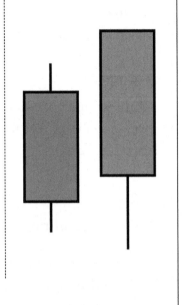

Would anyone like to hazard a guess as to whether Dark Cloud Cover is bullish or bearish?

I spotted a Dark Cloud Cover in the FTSE futures on 5 and 6 May 2006 (see Figure 4-5). At the time it was trading just above 6000. I warned that "a storm may be brewing" – never missing the opportunity to throw in a dodgy pun. I said at the time that I would look for a break back below 6000 before acting upon the reversal pattern though. I did this on 12 May, a day when the market sold off 117 points. Over the next 6 days the market sold off down to 5506, a near 500 point drop from our trigger level. I think the storm I predicted took place!

Another Dark Cloud Cover could be seen in the FTSE futures on the 15 and 18 June 2007 (Figure 4-6). Even if this book has a long shelf life and is still being read in many years to come, I think what happened in the summer of 2007 will still be remembered (will we ever forget the word subprime?), but just in case, I've posted the following chart – Figure 4-5 – as well as the chart for the reversal in 2007 – Figure 4-6.

Source: CQG, Inc. © 2008 All rights reserved worldwide.

Figure 4-5: FTSE 100 futures (all sessions, active unadjusted continuation); daily candlestick chart; 27 March 2006 – 26 May 2006, showing Dark Cloud Cover on 5/8 May 2006

When the market went on to break below 6000 I was ready to go short, and despite this being 150 ticks off the highs the market still sold off heavily subsequently.

Source: CQG, Inc. © 2008 All rights reserved worldwide.

Figure 4-6: FTSE 100 futures (all sessions, active unadjusted continuation); daily candlestick chart; 18 May 2007 – 31 July 2007, showing Dark Cloud Cover on 15/18 June 2007

This was followed by four red candles in a row, then a recovery of sorts. This mini-recovery lasted until mid July, but the market never retook the high from 18 June, and after a few days the selling commenced again in style.

Interestingly, in researching this book I spotted a Dark Cloud Cover example from 1985, again in the FTSE, in a book written by Elli Gifford (*The Investors Guide to Technical Analysis*, 1995), a former leading light of the UK Society of Technical Analysts. It seems that this isn't one to ignore if you're looking at the UK stock market!

Let's think about the psychology of this pattern briefly. The first day is a green candle in line with the bullish mode that's prevalent at the time. The first trade of the next day sees the market gapping higher, so at that time the bulls are once again flexing their muscles and looking totally in charge of the situation.

What happens for the rest of the day? The sellers dominate, that's what. The selling sees us give back a good proportion of the buying seen the previous day and the market closed *well into* the real body of the first candlestick. This is one of those times when it appears that the conversion from the Japanese textbooks on the subject hit upon some translation problems. Or is it that in the Western world we need everything defined to the *n*th degree? I've always had the impression with candlesticks that the Japanese appear to be happy to be a bit more visual, whereas we want things to be very clear cut and rules-based.

Introduction to the Marabuzo line

But something interesting has come of this. It's generally accepted that a close *well into* the first candle's real body for this pattern should be classed as below its halfway point.

There is a name in candlestick analysis for the halfway point of the real body of a large bodied candlestick, and it is the Marabuzo line. The next chapter is entirely devoted to this, so I won't get too involved here, except to say that to post a Dark Cloud Cover pattern we need the second candlestick to close below the Marabuzo line of the first candle.

To gap or not to gap – Dark Cloud Cover variations

The next thing worth talking about where this pattern is concerned is rule number 4: "The market gaps higher on the open of the second candle".

That means that the top of the real body of the second candle should be above the high of the first day (ie, above the top of the upper shadow). Quite often I see this rule disregarded, or is it misinterpreted? Let's not worry about that for a second; let's go through the issue.

Below I have posted two candlestick combinations.

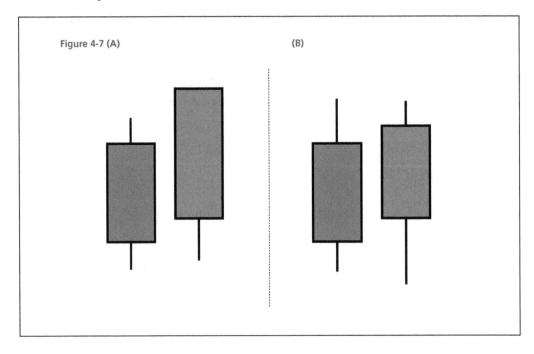

Figure 4-7 (A) (B)

In both cases there are two candles, the first of which is green. Figure A is a classic Dark Cloud Cover as it satisfies all of our rules set out on page 78. In Figure B you can see the market didn't open above the first day's high on the second day. It opened above the previous day's *close*, but not above the previous day's high, ie, it didn't gap higher.

I have often seen this combination called Dark Cloud Cover, and there's a strong argument that it doesn't matter where the market opened on the second day, the important thing is where the market closed on that day, which is the same in both instances. After all, it's the state of mind of the market at the end of the second candle that will dictate whether it is indeed in the throes of a reversal.

I prefer to call it a variation on a Dark Cloud Cover and to not ignore it entirely on that basis. We will look later at how flexibility can be, and at times has to be, applied to the reading of candlesticks.

The Poor Man's Engulfing Pattern?

If we assume that we're happy to class either of these situations as Dark Cloud Cover then it can be said that this is a Poor Man's Engulfing Pattern. After all, if we'd continued lower and posted a close below the first day's open we'd have posted a Bearish Engulfing Pattern, so surely Dark Cloud Cover is just a watered down version that didn't quite manage to do as much? Dark Cloud Cover can be regarded as a "nearly man"!

Whatever works

This is a valid argument, but once again brings us back to something I've touched upon before, something I like to call the "whatever works" rule. If you see Dark Cloud Cover formations at the top of every move on the chart that you use for your analysis then you shouldn't be discouraged because some textbook has told you they're not as strong as a Bearish Engulfing Pattern. I say again, I've often been asked to rate candlesticks with some sort of star rating according to how strong they are, and while there are patterns that should, in theory, be stronger than others, they can never be classed as guaranteed. As with anything to do with technicals, you have to do the work and you have to look back and see what works best on the chart you are viewing. You may find that Dark Cloud Cover patterns are excellent reversal patterns, just as they were in the FTSE in the charts we've looked at in this section. I'm certainly not going to ignore the next Dark Cloud Cover I see in the FTSE futures, just because it didn't make it as a Bearish Engulfing Pattern!

Dark Cloud Cover summary

Dark Cloud Cover is a marvellously gloomy sounding two candle reversal pattern seen during an uptrend. The first candle has an open real body and is in line with the bullish tone of the market. On the second day we see weakness after a strong start, and a close is posted well into the real body of the first candle. While it is generally not as strong as a Bearish Engulfing Pattern, I think the close on the second day below the Marabuzo line of the first candle should at the very least be treated with suspicion if you're long.

Piercing Pattern

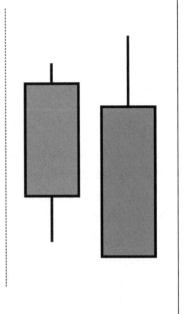

Piercing Pattern properties

BULLISH REVERSAL

1. Two candle pattern

2. The first candle has a filled real body, in line with the downtrend

3. The market gaps lower on the open of the second candle

4. The second candle has an open real body

5. The second candle's body closes 'well into' the real body of the first, ie, above the halfway mark of the first candle's real body

6. The market is in a **downtrend**

The opposite of Dark Cloud Cover is a Piercing Pattern, sometimes called the Piercing Line formation.

You can see these are a similar set of rules to the Dark Cloud Cover reversal, but turned on their head – this time it's a bullish pattern in a downtrending market because the bulls come storming back to life on the second day, and take back a good chunk of the losses seen in the previous session.

This all came on the back of a pretty shoddy start to proceedings on the second day. After the first candle, and on the open of the second candle, the bears were by far the happier group, and were dominating things. But then the market experienced strong buying which was sustained into the close, and an open bodied candle was posted.

If on the second session the bulls had kept up the good work and taken us above the open from the first day, and if these gains were sustained into the close a Bullish Engulfing Pattern would have been posted. Many argue therefore that the Piercing Pattern is a "nearly man" Engulfing pattern! Once again I'd echo my sentiments from a few pages back: if you find that a particular pattern works well on your charts, then don't mind me. Use it!

Source: CQG, Inc. © 2008 All rights reserved worldwide.

Figure 4–8: Anglo American plc; daily candlestick chart; 5 December 2007 – 18 February 2008, showing Piercing Pattern on 21 and 22 January 2008

Ideally the volume characteristics of a Piercing Pattern show a jump in volume on the second candle; in other words the buying that created the green candlestick was proper buying, and not just the result of the bears having a day off.

Piercing Pattern summary

A Piercing Pattern is two candlesticks, the first having a filled real body which is in line with the bearish conditions at the time. A candlestick with an open real body is then posted the next day, closing well into the red real body of the first candle. My personal experience is that Piercing Patterns are so few and far between that I always get a bit of a jolt when I see one. Once again this pattern's formation relies upon the second candle's close being well into the filled real body of the candle before it; our Marabuzo line comes into play once more, as a close below the Marabuzo line would mean no Piercing Pattern. This in itself can make these levels an important reference, as we'll discuss in the next chapter.

Bullish Harami

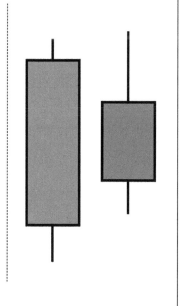

Bullish Harami properties

BULLISH REVERSAL

1. Two candle pattern

2. The first candle has a filled real body, in line with the downtrend

3. The second candle has an open real body that is contained within the filled real body of the candle before it

4. Shadows are of no concern; this pattern's construction is all about the real bodies

5. The market is in a **downtrend**

The next pattern we're going to look at is the Harami, which translates into English as "pregnant". The reason the Harami is so named is because the pattern involves two candles, one of which is contained within the other.

There are two types of Harami: bullish and bearish. We're going to start with the bullish version.

You know the routine by now, and hopefully you're already a step ahead of me in that you're already looking at our two candles and working out the price action involved, and how this direction of travel combines to suggest a reversal.

On the first day of our two candle pattern the market sells off, which is absolutely no surprise to man nor beast, as we're in a downtrend, and this is a pretty normal occurrence. What happens on the open of the second day is an instant clue to the potential reversal, as the market starts higher, within the previous day's range. This second session finishes with a smaller real body than the first day, although it is the opposite colour. So our green real body is contained within the red real body before it. Okay, so not much happened in the second session, but this in itself is better than what occurred the day before, and it shows that there's a potential change in the balance of power.

As a rule of thumb the Harami isn't the strongest of reversal patterns and you'd look for a bit more confirmation than with other patterns that we've already discussed. The reason the Harami gets such good airplay is that it's quite a common pattern.

Below is an example of a Bullish Harami in action in the Long Gilt. I saw the pattern (the candles circled at point D) and flagged it, but decided to wait until the market got through gap resistance overhead at 103.70 before I really believed in the idea that the pattern was reversing.

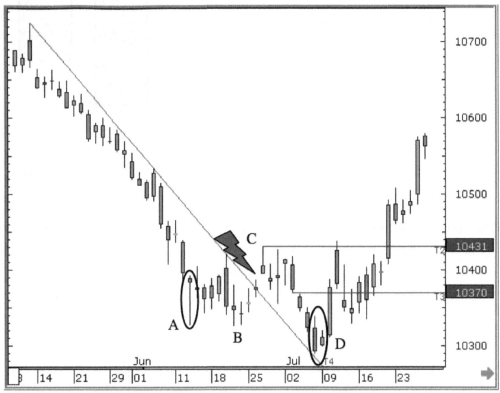

Source: CQG, Inc. © 2008 All rights reserved worldwide.

Figure 4–9: LIFFE Long Gilt futures (adjusted active continuation); daily candlestick chart; 9 May 2007 – 27 July 2007, showing Bullish Harami Pattern on 6 and 9 July 2008

We'd already been bitten once thinking that this one had reversed. If you look to the left of our Harami you'll see the Hammer pattern posted on 13 June (A). Subsequent to this the Hammer's low was held with a couple of small-bodied sessions at point B.

A few days later trend resistance was broken at point C (the thunderflash!) At this point it looked like the bulls were waking up, but again there was a failure to follow through and prices subsequently headed lower, until the Bullish Harami was posted at point D. At this point we needed to see the market take out the gap resistance at 103.70, which it did the next day, but the up-move only really got going after 104.31 was broken, which is the high at C.

Bullish Harami Pattern summary

A Bullish Harami Pattern is seen during a downtrending market and is made up of two candles. The first is a filled candle in line with the downtrend. The second is a candle with an open real body that sits within the confines of the filled real body of the first candle. The brakes have been put on the down-leg and although the second day doesn't show a strong reaction higher we have been warned and can now be more alert to any subsequent moves to a bull trend. It is often described as a mirror image of the Engulfing Pattern, but is generally nothing like as powerful. Not one of my favourites, but can be a good warning signal.

Bearish Harami

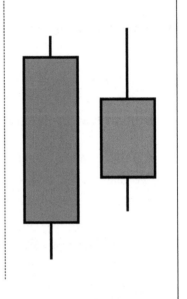

Bearish Harami properties

BEARISH REVERSAL

1. Two candle pattern

2. The first candle has an open real body, in line with an uptrend

3. The second candle has a filled real body that is contained within the real body of the open candle before it

4. Shadows are of no concern; this pattern's construction is all about the real bodies

5. The market is in an **uptrend**

The next line is going to be rather predictable, I fear. The opposite of a Bullish Harami is… can you guess? Yes indeed! Go to the top of the class! A Bearish Harami.

As you can see from our box on the previous page, it has all of the rules of the Bullish Harami but in reverse; this time a small red real body sits within the green real body prior to it.

In other words, day one was good for the bulls, and when you consider that we're in an uptrend this is no big shock to anyone. The weak open on the second day of our pattern is the first sign that the market may be struggling at these levels. The Bulls don't react to this weak open on this particular day. Often weakness in an uptrend is pounced upon as a buying opportunity by the bulls, if they're in a dominant mood. But that doesn't happen on this occasion. Instead the market does pretty much nothing, and ends the day within the real body of the previous session.

We're not worried about the shadows on this pattern, remember, we're only concerned with the position and size of the second real body, which must be a "baby" contained within the "mother" candle before it.

The reason why this is classed as a reversal is because the second session is a pathetic effort after all that's gone before. Usually it's accompanied by a failure to make a new high as well, and generally we'd ask for a bit more confirming price action subsequently before acting upon it.

If I were forced to give pattern star ratings based on my personal experience across all markets and time frames this one would score pretty lowly, although as I mentioned earlier this is not a game I like to play.

Source: CQG, Inc. © 2008 All rights reserved worldwide.

Figure 4-10: British Energy plc; daily candlestick chart; 15 November 2007 – 29 January 2008, showing Bearish Harami on 8/9 January 2008

If you looked back at the previous price history of this stock you would instantly have seen that £6.00 was a strong resistance level, so seeing a Harami when approaching this level would have piqued interest at least.

This wasn't the top on this occasion, as there were some decent gains the next day, when the market got through 600 to print 607, but on this day the gains were sold into and the session ended back near the lows, posting a Shooting Star. This was engulfed the next day with a big red candle. I've never quite decided what the collective noun for candlestick reversals should or could be, but I'd certainly be using it in this case. We have a gaggle of reversal patterns, a sloth of bears, a cacophony of noise arguing in favour of further downside, and the market duly obliged.

Spotting the Harami pattern would have given you an early hint that something was amiss, and with each day that another negative candlestick was posted our conviction increased. Once 5.50 cracked just one week after our Harami the market dropped another 85 pence in five days.

You were ready for this sort of move, and the Harami meant you'd "geared up" earlier than you might have done without it. So it wasn't a definitive reversal signal, but it still did a job for us.

The psychology behind the Harami is that the market opened weaker on the second day, immediately putting doubt into people's minds. As is customary in a strong uptrend, this weakness was not bought into. While it's fair to say the bears didn't exactly weigh in and change the entire landscape, there's still been a subtle change in the balance of power, with no one dominating the second day.

Bearish Harami summary

The Bearish Harami warns of a market topping out. It is constructed of two candles. The second candle has a filled real body, usually quite small, contained within the open real body before it.

It isn't one of my favourite patterns but can serve to set off a few alarm bells, which can be useful particularly if you're in a trade and wondering where or when to take some profit.

Candlesticks don't have to be a "black and white" signal generating tool!

This is something I often try to get across to people about candlesticks, especially people who want to be completely definitive about this sort of thing. There have been many studies done on technical analysis and candlesticks, and they always "do the stats". For example, you see a pattern and you buy it the next day and you run it for n number of days. If you did this with Harami patterns the results would probably be abysmal. If you did it with something supposedly more potent like Shooting Stars the results would almost certainly still be ordinary, if not disastrous.

The point I'm trying to get across right now though is that they don't have to be treated in this way at all. You can simply use candlesticks to give you a better understanding of the balance of power between bulls and bears at any particular moment, and you can use candlestick reversal patterns to set off alarms that maybe a move is running out of steam. At least then you'll be ready for a turn around.

It's so easy as a trader, and a chartist, to get married to a position, a trade or a trend. If you're making good money on something it's so easy to get carried away with the idea that it's going to last forever. This simply isn't going to be the case, and you don't want to maintain your long position all the way back down. Maybe something like a Bearish Harami reversal can jog you out of thinking that the market's going to go up for ever and always, and can have you getting ready to jump out of a position earlier than you normally would, before you give too much back.

Bearish Star

Bearish Star properties

BEARISH REVERSAL

1. Two candle pattern

2. The first candle has an open real body, in line with the Bull trend

3. The second candle's real body gaps away from the first candle's real body

4. The second candle has a small real body

5. The colour of the second candle's real body is not important

5. The market is in an **uptrend**

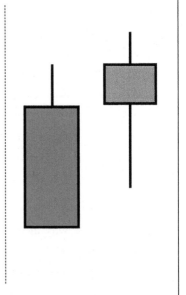

You could class the Star as a one candle pattern, but I have always been happier to call it a two candle pattern, and ask that a Star-like candle is posted after a strong up day. A Star is a small bodied candle that gaps away from a large bodied candle before it. The real body of the second candle doesn't have to be above the first candle's high, but this makes it more potent.

The point is that the second candlestick is small of real body, in other words it was a day where the bulls didn't beat the bears. It was a pretty even balance between the two, and all of that after such a promising start.

That's the key point behind the Star formation. The open on the second day was higher, so the bulls had a chance to show their stuff, but they didn't. We ended up having a damp squib of a session. It's almost the same sort of psychology as a Harami, except this time there was an added bit of bullishness first up in that there was early promise on day 2. This early promise didn't translate into another solid day. The bears did as well as the bulls, and no one won. Have things changed? Has the balance evened out? Did the bulls mess up what started out as a really promising session for them? Quite possibly the answer to all of these questions is "Yes!"

On the first trading day of 2008, NYMEX Light Sweet Crude hit $100. The London-based Brent Crude Oil contract didn't quite make this mark, trading up to 98.50 on a day that ended with a small bodied candle that gapped away from the big green candle before it, or in other words, a Star.

As you can see the market sold off a bit the next day (which actually engulfed the previous day), but it took a few more days before things really got going for the bears and within a few weeks the market had pulled back to 85.00, where a bounce was seen after a Hammer day.

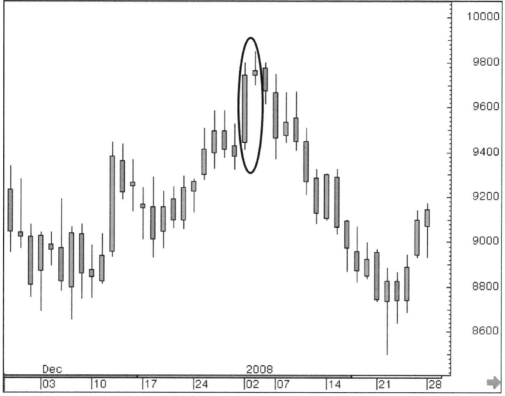

Source: CQG, Inc. © 2008 All rights reserved worldwide.

Figure 4-11: ICE Brent Crude Oil futures (all sessions, unadjusted continuation chart); daily candlestick chart; 28 November 2007 – 28 January 2008

Now here's something that I've always said about Star days.

What are the headlines in the press the next day? "Oil hits new all time highs" and "Oil nudging $100" are the sorts of thing that we would have seen after this day, all trumpeting from the rooftops that the market is at levels never before seen, and surely $200 is the next stop!

Most technicians recognise that round numbers can make important psychological barriers, and therefore form support or resistance levels. I believe that most find this a bit difficult to grasp, because these round number levels are surely the sort of thing that only private investors and less sophisticated investors would be looking at, whereas surely the smart money shouldn't care about such frivolities? But be assured, these levels do count for some reason, so shouldn't be ignored.

Anyway I digress. After the day that oil (in the US at least) hit $100 the whole world was talking about how much higher it could go, but anyone trading Brent who looked at the daily candlestick chart on that day should have at least scratched his or her cranium. This is what I wrote the next day:

> *'As you can see from the chart this mixed session left us with a small bodied candlestick. This should be used as a warning sign of the bull run waning.'*

In the next section (Evening Star) I'll come back to this, as there's a bit more to say.

Bearish Star summary

A Bearish Star is a small bodied candle seen above a large open bodied candle in a rising market. The small body on the second day shows that despite a promising start the bulls lost temporary control. We should now be on alert in case this loss of control becomes a more sustained deal from the bears, ie, a reversal.

You can also get Stars in bear markets, warning that a down-leg may be cooling off or even reversing, so now we'll look at the Bullish Star.

Bullish Star

Bullish Star properties

BULLISH REVERSAL

1. Two candle pattern
2. The first candle has a filled real body, in line with the Bear trend
3. The second candle's real body opens lower and gaps away from the first candle's real body
4. The second candle has a small real body
5. The colour of the second candle's real body is not important
5. The market is in a **downtrend**

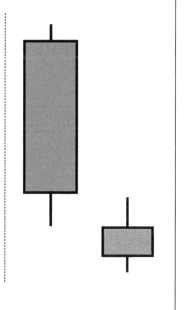

If the market is in a downtrend and you see a small bodied candle immediately after a big red one this may be a sign that the downtrend is on the wane. If this candle was seen within the previous red candle's real body it would be a Harami, however if the second, small bodied candle gaps lower with a bad start it's called a Star.

The bears are in charge because the market is in a downtrend, and the big lower open is just further proof that the bears are doing all the bossing. But if this great start from the sellers doesn't see any subsequent "oomph" then we should start to get concerned that maybe the bears are losing the will or the ability to keep it going.

Source: CQG, Inc. © 2008 All rights reserved worldwide.

Figure 4-12: Shire Pharmaceuticals Group plc; daily candlestick chart; 26 November 2007 – 26 February 2008, showing several Star combinations

Figure 4-12 shows three Bullish Stars. The first didn't work at all. There was absolutely no subsequent confirmation, and therefore I wouldn't have taken this signal.

The second saw the market gap quite a bit lower on the Star day, and it then rallied into the close to post a green real body (remember though, the colour of the real body is not that important for this pattern, although obviously the close at the top of the day's range in this instance may well have added some conviction). As you can see I got some instant gratification on this occasion with a strong up day the next day.

But the rally soon petered out and the market decided to come back and fill the gap seen after our Star formation (see Chapter 5 for a discussion of gaps). In doing this another Star pattern was formed, and this time there was a decent rally for several sessions after the gap-filling Star.

Summary

If you are in a strong downtrend you will likely see a fair few big down days posted, with large filled real bodies. If after one of these the market opens significantly lower but then does nothing for the rest of the day, this lack of reaction can be taken as a warning signal that the selling is stalling.

So we can see that the Star patterns that work the best are the ones where there's confirmation subsequently, which sets the scene nicely for the next pair of patterns: the Morning and Evening Stars.

Evening Star

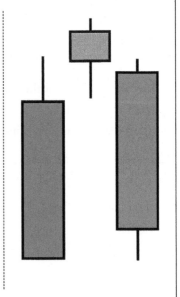

Evening Star properties

BEARISH REVERSAL

1. Three candle pattern

2. The first candle has an open real body, in line with the Bull trend

3. The second candle's real body gaps away from the first candle's real body

4. The second candle has a small real body

5. The colour of the second candle's real body is not important

6. The third candle is filled and closes well into the real body of the first candle

5. The market is in an **uptrend**

An Evening Star is a three candle pattern, but if you've just read the previous few pages, understanding it will be a very simple task, as all we're doing is adding one more element to a Bearish Star – an immediate confirming candle.

So there are two candles that make up a Bearish Star – a green candle followed by a small candle that gaps higher. After a really good start on day two nothing really happened, and I was raising an eyebrow that the bulls didn't keep things going. Then the third day is a big red candle that confirms the suspicions expressed after the small gap day. The third day sees the market close well into the real body of the first candle of the three.

Once again we see that phrase "well into" with regard to the closing value of the third candlestick. Where have we seen this before? If you go back to the section on Dark Cloud Cover you'll see that for the formation to be completed the second candle's body has to see a close well into the real body of the first's. We solve this slight ambiguity by using the Marabuzo line of the first candle, and the same applies here: we need to see a close on the third day below the halfway point, or Marabuzo line, of the real body of the first candle of the pattern.

The Japanese particularly favour these patterns, and you can see why – there are three key elements needed to make up the reversal:

1. Initial strength

2. A day of pure indecision despite the market making a new high

3. A session that backs up the indecisiveness of the previous session and confirms that prices had reached levels that were too high!

It is a recurring theme when you study Japanese charting techniques that the number three has almost mystical connotations. Maybe this is what makes Evening and Morning Stars so potent, it's because they show a reversal occurring over three different candles. There are many other patterns in candlestick analysis with "three" in their name: three upside gaps, three red soldiers, rising/falling three methods, and three Buddha tops and bottoms (akin to the Western Head & Shoulders pattern).

Examples

Source: CQG, Inc. © 2008 All rights reserved worldwide.

Figure 4-13: Astra Zeneca plc; daily candlestick chart; 29 January 2007 – 8 May 2007, showing Evening Star on 19, 20, 23 April 2007

You can see on the left hand side that the market had got to within a whisker of the psychologically important £30 level on a couple of occasions, but then was faced with some weakness. The market rallied again though, several times, and in April saw a run higher that ended with an Evening Star. The day after the Evening Star had been completed the market gapped lower, and sold off over 5% in the next 8 sessions – instant gratification!

This proves something else about these powerful reversal patterns. Even though this pattern's formation involved the market selling off just under 5% from the high, there was still plenty of weakness immediately afterwards to make money on the short side. It's never too low to sell, nor – in a rising market – too high to buy.

Abandoned babies

This illustrates an ideal world scenario for an Evening Star pattern, with the middle candle sitting pretty on its own above the rest of the chart. In fact there is a name for a small bodied candle that sits on the chart after having gapped higher (or lower in a downtrend, below the rest of the market). It's called an Abandoned Baby.

This is one of those patterns where as soon as you start to talk about it you start to get those "I think he may be losing his marbles" looks.

Variation – no gap on the open of day three

The cynics among you may argue at this point that we don't live in an ideal world, and even when I'm in my most optimistic of moods I have to concur! Nevertheless as long as we stick to the basic principles, there are several combinations of candles that can come together and still be classed as an Evening Star. The following chart shows a variation that I would be happy to call an Evening Star, even though the market didn't gap lower on the third day. The important message about the third session, surely, is where it finished? Even if the market didn't gap lower at the start of this session, surely the selling that followed was enough to make you at least worry that things might be changing? The psychology of the third session of an Evening Star is all about how far the sellers took us back into the range of the first day, not where the first trade of the day may have been.

Source: CQG, Inc. © 2008 All rights reserved worldwide.

Figure 4-14: Diageo plc; daily candlestick chart; 9 May 2007 – 3 August 2007, showing variation on an Evening Star posted on 15, 18 and 19 June

When candle patterns collide

There's something else that can be said about the Diageo chart shown in Figure 4-14. The second and third candles of the Evening Star also combine to form a variation on a Bearish Engulfing Pattern. Although the real body of the first candle (of the Engulfing Pattern, the middle candle of the Evening Star) wasn't open, the next candle certainly satisfied any criteria for being classed as Engulfing. You may have noticed that I am sneaking into the text the idea of adopting some flexibility into the reading of the charts and the patterns. This is quite deliberate, although there are some observers (particularly the left brain people) who would strongly disagree with this blurring of the lines.

To those people I would ask the following question: in a real life situation would you want to ignore a big sell-off day at a high like the one we can see in the Diageo chart? This can be classed as an Evening Star, a Bearish Engulfing Pattern, a Tweezer Top or a Bearish Belt Hold Line to name but a few!

Maybe though, the point isn't what we should call it, but what we would do about it in a live situation, and whichever way you look at it, it wasn't the best of sessions for the bulls. It came right on a high, it was a big down day, and it didn't take long for the market to start to confirm it subsequently. If you were long and you allowed the bearish candles to signal some lightening up of your position, you would have been delighted. If you had sold the market short after the formation of the pattern you would have only been showing a loss for a short period of time during the subsequent session.

Merging candles

If you are in a strong downtrend you will likely see a fair few big down days posted, with large filled real bodies. If after one of these the market opens significantly lower but then does nothing for the rest of the day, this lack of reaction can be taken as a warning signal that the selling is stalling.

So we can see that the Star patterns that work the best are the ones where there's confirmation subsequently, which sets the scene nicely for the next pair of patterns: the Morning and Evening Stars.

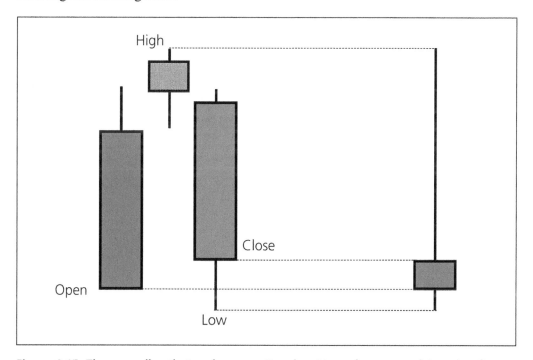

Figure 4-15: Three candles that make up an Evening Star, when merged together form a Shooting Star

Evening Star summary

An Evening Star is a powerful reversal pattern seen in a rising market. It is comprised of three candles. The first is a bullish day, the second is a Star with indecision rife despite the early promise. This indecision turns into outright bearishness on day three, which is why this is such a powerful reversal, and so closely watched by the Japanese.

You may have an idea where we're going to go next on our trawl through the candlestick patterns. What happens when a Bullish Star formation is backed up by a strong day the next day? You've got it!

Morning Star

Morning Star properties

BULLISH REVERSAL

1. Three candle pattern

2. The first candle has a filled real body, in line with the weak trend

3. The second candle's real body gaps lower, away from the first candle's real body

4. The second candle has a small real body

5. The colour of the second candle's real body is not important

6. The third candle is open and it finishes well into the real body of the first candle

5. The market is in a **downtrend**

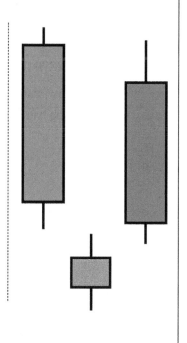

It's a pretty simple step to go from a Bullish Star to a Morning Star: you just need a nice big open candle to make it a three candle pattern – the third day confirms the suspicions aroused when the market stopped travelling relentlessly lower the previous day (the middle day of the three).

The buyers are back in town, and day two was the definitive turning point. The market has moved in a "V" shape over the three days. It's all change.

As I said with the Evening Star, this is a particularly potent pattern according to the Japanese, and you can see why. There are lots of components that need to come together, and ticking all the boxes requires a pretty serious turnaround in the market's fortunes.

Third day flexibility

I've always subscribed to the view that the starting point of the third day is of far less importance than where it ends, so I don't worry about whether the market gaps higher on the third session. Instead, only the condition of closing well into the real body of the first day needs to be satisfied (that word Marabuzo comes into play once more).

So Figure 4-16 below shows an ideal scenario Morning Star, and Figure 4-17 shows a variation that we'd be happy to label as such.

Examples

Source: CQG, Inc. © 2008 All rights reserved worldwide.

Figure 4-16: Anglo American plc; weekly candlestick chart; 28 August 2007 – 28 April 2008, showing Morning Star pattern between 14 January and 1 February 2008

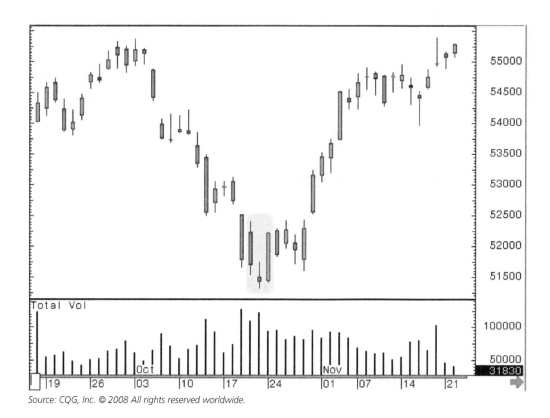

Source: CQG, Inc. © 2008 All rights reserved worldwide.

Figure 4-17: FTSE futures (unadjusted continuation); daily candlestick chart; 16 Sep 2005 – 22 Nov 2005, showing Morning Star variation on 20, 21 and 24 October 2005

Combining the Morning Star

Again we would pose the question of what these three candles would become if you were to condense them all together into one? Hopefully you can see how price action that takes on a "V" shape can form a reversal pattern however long it takes, be it one day or three days. The following illustration shows this clearly.

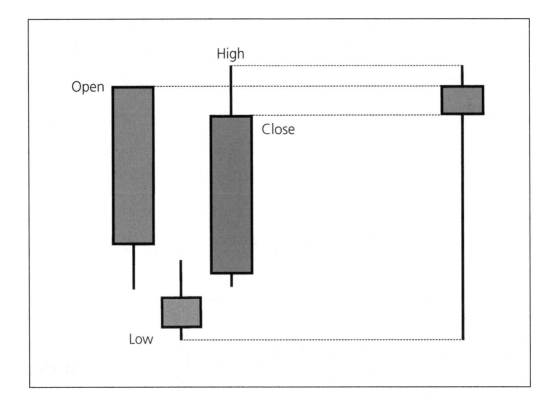

Figure 4-18: Three candles that make up a Morning Star – when merged together they form a Hammer

Morning Star summary

The three candles that form a Morning Star make a potent argument for the reversal of an established downtrend. The first candle has a large filled real body just like many of the other sessions that we've seen during the downtrend. Day two starts off with further weakness but then nothing really happens. After this questions should be asked as to the sustainability of the down-move. Day three answers these questions. A big open candle tells us the bulls are back in town.

The importance of the Marabuzo line to most of these patterns

In looking at the Dark Cloud Cover, Piercing Patterns, and Morning and Evening Stars you have been introduced to the concept of the Marabuzo line, a level that defines when prices are moving well into the real body of a preceding candlestick. Prices need to break through this level to form these patterns, and it needs to do so on a closing basis.

An Evening Star isn't an Evening Star if the third candlestick in the trio doesn't close below the Marabuzo line of the first. Similarly a Dark Cloud Cover formation is only formed when weakness on the second session takes us below the Marabuzo line of the green candle posted beforehand. Of course this weakness also has to be maintained into the close, but the breaking of this level has to occur first, and this very often sees these levels becoming a strong focus.

Marabuzo lines for reversal rejection and trend confirmation

Marabuzo lines can also be excellent "lines in the sand" if you want to confirm a reversal pattern, even if they're not required in the set of rules. For example, I said in the last chapter that Harami generally aren't the strongest of reversal patterns, and that a bit of extra confirmation is always good in this situation. Have a look at the following chart:

Source: CQG, Inc. © 2008 All rights reserved worldwide.

Figure 4–19: ICE Brent Crude Oil futures (all sessions, unadjusted continuation); daily candlestick chart; 4 September 2007 – 6 November 2007

Two Bearish Harami patterns were posted in a row on 16 and 17 October, then again on 18 and 19 October. Only a few days earlier, on 15 October, a big green candle with a Marabuzo line at 81.50 was posted. Looking back at my commentary after these Harami patterns, we see that the reversal patterns were flagged, but I asked that the market take out 81.50 before becoming too concerned that a change of trend was taking place.

The power of the Marabuzo line came into play again a week or so later. You can see a big red candle was posted at point A (30 October 2007). This was one of the most bearish days the oil markets had ever seen in absolute terms (at the time), but I went into the next day sticking with a bull stance, because the market hadn't broken 86.12, the Marabuzo line from the big open candle posted on 25 October 2007.

In fact I said on the very next day that if 86.12 held, one should be using the weakness as a buying opportunity. Needless to say I was very pleased to see the low of the day coming in at 86.13, followed by a very swift rally that swept away any of the worries created by the previous session.

So I'm happy to put a Marabuzo line on any large bodied candlestick because I've noted over the years that these can be extremely good support or resistance levels over the next day or two – or sometimes for even longer.

Just for the sake of clarity, below is a good example of Marabuzo lines proving to be a good reference to stay with the bears in a down move.

Source: CQG, Inc. © 2008 All rights reserved worldwide.

Figure 4-20: LIFFE Long Gilt futures (adjusted continuation); daily candlestick chart; 17 March 2008 – 23 May 2008

One thing worth noting at this point is that these lines generally work best if they give support in an uptrend or resistance in a downtrend. Let's go through all of these conditions for clarification purposes.

If the market is in a solid uptrend you will see many strong days with large green candles. After these big up days we are generally left looking at a big green real body to which we can apply a Marabuzo line. Any weakness in the subsequent days often finds support at these lines. Think about it; in an uptrending market you should be looking for buying opportunities, or support levels where the buyers are likely to step back in. I always suggest looking to trade in the direction of the underlying trend, for example buying dips to support in rising markets. Unless you have extremely deep pockets it's far better to try and position yourself in line with this. It's much easier to walk out of a train terminal during the rush hour than into the station, because you're going along with the tide of the crowd, and not trying to push against it.

If you're in a downtrend and looking for selling opportunities you could do worse than short the market at the Marabuzo line of a big red candle, as the example on the previous page shows clearly.

Psychology of Marabuzo lines

What's the psychology that makes Marabuzo lines so effective? I think there may be something about halfway that makes people sit up and pay attention. I've never run a marathon but I know a few people that have, and they all said that the 13 mile mark is an important one: knowing you're halfway round gives you a boost. I feel like that most Wednesday lunchtimes!

Once prices get back above the Marabuzo line of a big red candle in a downtrending market, the bulls feel like they've achieved something. This is a rarity at the time, of course! The bears who defended this level, and possibly used it as a selling opportunity, have been wrong-footed and need to buy back to stop out. There may have been bears who weren't going to worry about their short positions unless some key resistances started being retaken. The Marabuzo line would be one such key resistance, so its break may cause these shorts to start covering.

Marabuzo lines summary

To sum up, I think Marabuzo lines can be a great tool for answering those big questions that are posed after large directional days.

Debt markets often see a strong reaction to the US Employment report on the first Friday of every month. The Monday after can often be a day of head-scratching as people try to decide whether the big move seen on the Friday should be followed by more of the same, or whether it was just a bit of over-reaction ("surely markets don't over-react?" he asked sarcastically).

Marabuzo lines can often answer this question. Say the market saw a strong reaction to the numbers and rallied from an open at 116.00 to a close of 118.00 on the Bonds. The

Marabuzo line will be at 117.00. We can say that all the time the market remains above 117.00 we can feel comfortable with the idea that the gains can be sustained and that the market is heading higher. However, if prices fall back through 117.00 maybe Friday's gains were overcooked, and in the cold light of day the sellers have been presented with an opportunity.

I have found over the years that these lines can provide extremely powerful and reliable levels of support or resistance, particularly in strongly trending markets.

5

Continuation Patterns

Rising/Falling Three Method and gaps

Introduction

Our voyage of discovery has so far concentrated purely on patterns that suggest the market may be turning over or reversing. These are the most powerful patterns in candlesticks but they are by no means the be all and end all. There are a bunch of patterns that signal a continuation of a trend, indicating that things have taken a temporary pause for breath before continuing on their merry way. This is often a difficult thing to decide: is a market merely retracing, or are we seeing a reversal? This is why I always ask for a bit more confirmation of any reversal pattern. The old phrase "one swallow doesn't make a summer" is quite relevant to candlestick analysis, I've always felt.

We've already, in the previous chapter, explored the use of Marabuzo lines to confirm or question any potential reversal. I personally like to also use things like a trend line or a reliable moving average; this is something we'll explore a bit later.

I don't want to spend too much time on continuation patterns because I've always found them to be rather obvious, especially once you are proficient at the exercise of getting inside the components of the individual candles you're viewing. To prove this point I've chosen the "rising/falling three" pattern as the topic of this section.

Falling or Rising Three Method

A Rising Three pattern is a continuation pattern in a falling market, where you see three small candles rising within the range of a previous red real body. In other words you see one great big down day followed by three rather meek up sessions, but the rises seen collectively over the three sessions don't do enough to repair the damage done on the first day. We're not quite done with this pattern because a fifth candlestick is needed to complete the picture: another big red candle that signals a resumption of the down move after our three counter trend candles.

So, a five candle pattern then! Wow! However, the psychology is, I think you'll agree, pretty simple to follow. We have a market that's in a downtrend and day one is just another typical session, dominated by the bears. Three days are then spent with prices gently nudging higher, but not with any real conviction.

This could be the result of some short covering. Or it could be that the big red candle was the result of a big bit of news, which was swiftly followed by a few days of calm after the storm reflection. Generally the market's first reaction to news flow is pretty reliable though, and after a few days of pondering, the realisation hits that this thing really needs selling again! The fifth day is the day that the market realises that the middle three sessions haven't made any real difference even if there has been some sort of recovery. Another big red candle proves that the bears are back in the box seat.

The Falling Three is the opposite, and is to do with the bulls taking a breather in an uptrend. As long as major support levels don't crack there's a good chance that the bulls will be reinvigorated at some point; after three days of sitting on the sidelines they decide enough is enough, and pile back in. The chart in Figure 5-1 shows an example of such a pause for breath on an intra-day chart.

Source: CQG, Inc. © 2008 All rights reserved worldwide.

Figure 5-1: CAC 40 futures (May 2008); 10-minute candlestick chart; 15 May 2008, 10.30am – 5.50pm

Gaps (or windows, to use the candlestick parlance)

What is a gap?

Even before I discovered candlesticks I always used to look at gaps, and I am a firm believer that they're something that cannot be ignored, particularly for day traders. While they're not strictly a continuation pattern, I do believe that they are best used to find support in an established uptrend and resistance in a down move, and in doing so they do a nice job of flagging a market that's happy to continue the trend it's in.

I will stick with what I'm used to, and continue to talk about gaps for this section, even though the traditional candlestick name is a "window".

A gap, quite simply, is an area of price at which no trade has taken place due to exceptionally strong, or exceptionally weak opens.

An open above the previous day's high creates a gap, and the previous day's high becomes gap support.

If, on the other hand, a market receives bad news and opens below the previous candle's low an upside gap is created (above the market) with gap resistance set at the top of the area of no trade, ie, at the low of the previous day's candle.

There are quite a few rules that I've heard over the years pertaining to gaps. For example, I have heard many times the theory that 80% of all gaps get filled within four days of their creation. In other words the market invariably goes back down to a gap support, or returns higher to a gap resistance, shortly after the gap appears.

In certain markets (one that springs to mind is Bund), you hear people say "it always fills the gap". A backtest shows this to be very close to the truth, although not 100%.

This book, being a broad brush introduction, will not go into the nuts and bolts of testing theories in this way. There has been plenty of testing done, with various degrees of reality involved, and it's a huge subject.

Instead what I will say is that gaps usually create quite a stir, and are often strong reference points, especially for those trading short-term time frames.

Why are gaps so important as a continuation signal in an uptrend?

If you open strongly and leave a gap below you have an instant support level. The bulls have a strong line in the sand and often buyers will put bids in at or ahead of the gap to try and gain good trade entry at what should be a key juncture.

If you gap higher in a solid uptrend this presents a potential "buy on a dip" opportunity in line with the trend, and therefore it has a better chance of doing its job.

If, again during an uptrend, the market falls through a gap, then maybe the bulls aren't as powerful as the overall trend suggests: maybe things are changing.

If you think about the Dark Cloud Cover formation and (not necessarily always, but quite often) the Bearish Engulfing Pattern, it is often the failure to hold the overnight gap that is the first sign of trouble. Obviously to form these patterns the bears have to do more work once they've taken us through the overnight gap support, but at least you're already alert to the possibility that things are weakening.

Gaps in a downtrending market

If a market opens below the previous day's low there is a gap to fill to the upside. The dominant bears often line up to sell at or just in front of this level, so you can see how the resistance is created.

A downtrending market that stays below an upside gap is showing its lack of upside conviction and proves that the bear tack should be stuck with. The market just doesn't want to go up.

If a security has been dropping sharply and gaps have been left to the upside then every time one of these key resistance levels is retaken on any subsequent rally the bulls have reason to cheer. It's something akin to a list of black marks being removed from the copybook.

So, as with Marabuzo lines, gaps are a simple yet highly effective way of gleaning support and resistance levels from our charts, and in turn the market's mood can be gauged, depending on whether these levels are holding or breaking.

This is particularly important in candlestick analysis because it is inherently a contrarian form of analysis. Spotting reversal patterns is key, so you need to see some confirmation after such a pattern. The immediate reaction to a reversal is to ask the market to "prove it!"

The traditional Western view on gaps

In Western analysis it's often suggested that there are different types of gap:

1. A breakaway gap signalling the start of a move

2. A measuring gap seen halfway through a trend (if you know where halfway is you can measure where the end should or could be)

3. An exhaustion gap, seen when a powerful trend (particularly an uptrend) is ending.

I like two out of the three of these. Let's go through them one by one to see why.

In my trading lifetime I have seen many breakaway gaps. I can also see the logic behind it, or the psychology if we want to stick to the underlying theme of this book. Often a stock goes on a run because someone tips it in the weekend press, or a strong piece of fundamental news is released, such as a pharmaceutical company getting approval for a new drug or a mining company striking a new vein, or a company receiving a takeover approach. All of these things can cause a market to gap higher and trigger the start of a bull run.

Similarly a breakaway gap can be seen at the start of a downtrend if a stock is downgraded, or if a bid is pulled, or if a drug is kyboshed by the FDA!

Exhaustion gaps are often seen at the end of big moves, when the market is entering the "silly season" stage; if these gaps start to show, you can instantly allow the alarm bells to start ringing. However, it is really only in retrospect that you can definitively label these as exhaustion gaps. At the time they may have that look and feel, but they are quite tough to trade, as you're batting against a strong move.

You only have to hear some of the rubbish that's written about markets when they're steaming higher. At the top of the dotcom bubble in 2000 your plumber was giving stock recommendations. "You can't lose" is a phrase that starts getting bandied about. Of course an old adage that makes far more sense is the one about "if it sounds too good to be true, it probably is."

Anyway, as soon as this sort of thing is occurring at a high, it's a sign that silly season has definitely arrived; the mania type buying is going to dry up quickly and the market will fall over very fast at some point. Sanity will be restored some time soon in the shape of a big reversal – a down-move that, at the very least, restores things to more sensible levels and gets rid of the froth.

Measuring, or halfway, gaps I just don't get. I also haven't seen much evidence of them, even if I haven't spent years religiously backtesting them. For the sake of completion, despite my dismissal a measuring gap is said to be seen at the mid point of a move. Once you know where the middle is, you can measure where the end could be.

Example

Below is one chart that will demonstrate many of the points discussed.

Source: CQG, Inc. © 2008 All rights reserved worldwide.

Figure 5-2: Eurex DAX futures (unadjusted continuation); daily candlestick chart; 26 November 2007 – 27 May 2008

It could be argued that the gap at point A was an exhaustion gap. But how would an observer know that at the time? It wouldn't be possible because it's only in hindsight that it can be classed as an exhaustion gap. But at the time all we know is that it should be a strong support on any pullbacks, and if the market fails to hold the gap on the way back down we get a hint of what's to come. Sure enough, once this gap failed to hold there was not much upside, and it was at this point it became apparent that it could have been an exhaustion deal. On the subsequent down move the market left a couple of gaps at B and C, and the day after gap C posted an enormous down day.

The gap at point D turned out to be an exhaustion gap for the downside move. It was bang in the middle of a Morning Star formation and a few days later the market gapped higher at point E. This gap held on a sell-off a few days later and provided a nice buying opportunity if you were looking for such a move on the back of the Morning Star.

At point F there was another gap that held on a couple of subsequent occasions in the ensuing weeks.

So you can see that gaps can signal the end or the beginning of trends, but the thing I really like is when they're in line with the unfolding trend. If you had sold the market on the open after gaps B and C, with a stop order above the gap, you would have had a trade with excellent risk/reward and a clear line in the sand to reference as far as getting out was concerned.

Chapter summary

Gaps can be extremely important reference points, and in my experience they work very well when seen in line with a firm trend, except in conditions where the market is capitulating, in which case they can be used as a warning of a potential reversal.

Often you will see a reversal pattern at an extreme after the market has left a gap or two. The gaps can be good reference points subsequently, to be used as confirmation of the reversals.

6

The Real World – Practical Application

Different time frames

Discovering your time frame: longer-term traders and money managers

"So what time frame charts should I use, then?" is a question I am often asked. My answer is always the same: "You need to work that out for yourself."

So far in this book we have discussed the common candlestick patterns by mostly viewing daily charts, where each candlestick represents a day's data.

We have seen a few examples of weekly charts, like the chart for Euro/USD with all the Hammers on it (Figure 3-3).

Daily and weekly candlestick charts can be used for making investment decisions with a time horizon of anything from two weeks upwards. When I say "time horizon" I mean the time frame for holding a position. Long-term buy and hold fund managers use longer-term charts; there's no point in them looking at intra-day charts as the apparent volatility could spook them into making rash decisions. They need a view of the bigger picture, and weekly charts do exactly this.

Many money managers use longer-term moving averages, the most common being the 50-day and 200-day averages, and I would suggest overlaying candlesticks onto these, looking for times when reversal patterns appear after a pullback to a reliable moving average line.

Source: CQG, Inc. © 2008 All rights reserved worldwide.

Figure 6-1: S&P 500 futures (unadjusted continuation); daily candlestick chart; 31 March 2004 – 23 June 2004, showing a Hammer on 12 May and a Bullish Harami on 17 and 18 May, both on the 200-day moving average line

As well as this I would suggest longer-term investors might look out for situations where there are candlestick reversal patterns appearing on weekly and daily charts at the same time. Opposite is a great example of this kind of thing, occurring at a top in the Long Gilt.

Source: CQG, Inc. © 2008 All rights reserved worldwide.

Figure 6-2a: LIFFE Long Gilt (adjusted continuation); daily candlestick chart; 9 November 2005 – 14 March 2006, showing 17, 18 and 19 January 2006 Evening Star

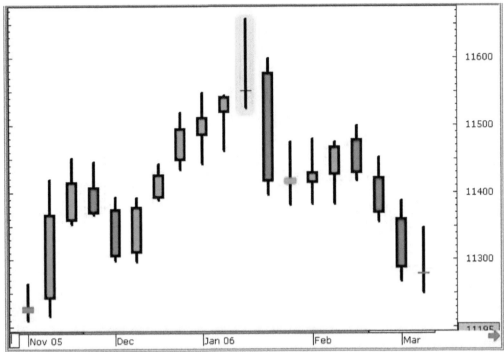

Source: CQG, Inc. © 2008 All rights reserved worldwide.

Figure 6-2b: LIFFE Long Gilt (adjusted continuation); weekly candlestick chart; 9 November 2005 – 14 March 2006, showing Long Legged Doji for the week of 16-20 January 2006

Most of the time that I see technical analysis being used by long-term money managers it is as a filtering process. You apply a set of conditions to a list of stocks or markets and ask a computer to give you a list of constituents of said list that tick all of your conditions. It is fairly simple these days to add pattern recognition into this sort of programme, so that you can make candlesticks a part of the process.

Say you have a filtering process that looks for stocks on the LSE that are below their 10-day moving average but have just hit their 200-day average. This may produce a list of, say, 50 stocks a day. If this is too many, then you need another parameter to narrow the search. How about stocks that at the same time post a candlestick reversal pattern? This is all very simplistic, but this is an introductory book, so I'm merely trying to provide a bit of food for thought. What you would then have is a list of stocks that have been selling off in the short term but are now hitting key long-term support and showing signs of reversing.

Ichimoku Charts

There is an increasing following for Ichimoku charts in longer-term decision making. It's a very simple box to tick to ask that something is above the Ichimoku Cloud on the weekly and daily charts before a buy signal is classed as confirmed. My STA colleague Nicole Elliott has written a fine book on the subject and in the UK we're also lucky enough to have another strong exponent of the subject (again, an active member of the STA) in David Linton.

Ichimoku charts are overlaid on a candlestick chart – the two go hand in hand.

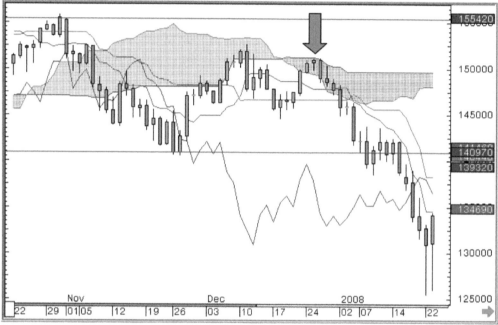

Source: CQG, Inc. © 2008 All rights reserved worldwide.

Figure 6-3: S&P 500 futures (unadjusted continuation); daily candlestick chart overlaid with Ichimoku; 22 October 2007 – 23 January 2008

At the end of December an Evening Star with a Hanging Man for a middle candle was posted (highlighted with the purple down arrow). This was seen within the cloud, with the top of the cloud capping upside on the pattern. A few days later when the market sold off through the bottom of the cloud the downside accelerated dramatically.

Discovering your time frame: shorter-term time frame traders

Daily charts can be used by all participants to keep a firm grip on the market's overall direction, and any suspected changes, from longer-term players right down to intra-day traders who are executing many trades per day. It's this group I want to talk about now because they can (and many actively do) use candlestick charts of all different time frames, down to 1-minute intervals if they're trading products that are liquid enough (although I'm not a big fan of going this short-term, personally – I don't like to view anything less than a 10-minute chart).

If you are a day trader wanting to use short-term candlestick charts as the basis, or even as just one element of your trading strategy, then I would like first of all to stress one very important thing: **Make viewing the daily and weekly charts for the instrument(s) you're trading a compulsory part of your daily routine.**

Warning!

I've seen many traders get so involved in the short-term price action that they forget the bigger picture. Candle charts, even daily and weekly charts, are *dynamic*, and can change without you even realising it. A potential reversal pattern can creep up on you, believe me!

Seeing the bigger picture can also help you to trade in the direction of the prevailing trend, and you should find making money easier if you're not trying to battle against the crowd every time you put a trade on. "The trend is your friend" is an old adage that's used in technical analysis and trader circles, and it's often greeted with a groan, but it's so much easier to make money in a falling market by going short than trying to pick the bottom.

But back to the short-term time frames: look at the two charts on the following pages. Both show similar-looking down moves followed by similar-looking up moves after the appearance of similar-looking Hammers, wouldn't you agree? Except Figure 6-4 is a daily candlestick chart, showing 35 days worth of data with a price range of $13.50, whereas Figure 6-5 is a 10-minute chart showing around eight hours worth of price action over a 79 tick range.

The Hammer in Figure 6-4 therefore took a whole day to form. In other words, over the course of an entire session the market sold off from 87.38 to 85.00 then rallied again, all the way back up to a high of 88.86, closing the day just shy of this high at 88.25.

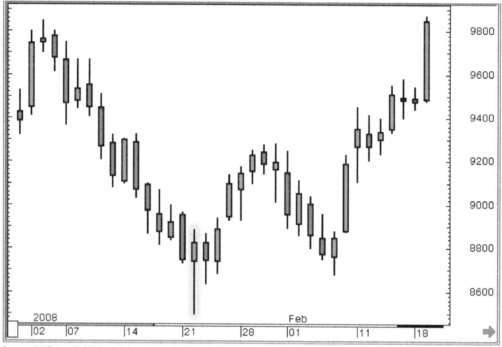

Source: CQG, Inc. © 2008 All rights reserved worldwide.

Figure 6-4: ICE Brent Crude Oil futures (all sessions, unadjusted continuation); daily candlestick chart; 31 December 2007 – 19 February 2008

This turned out to be the low of this move and over the course of the next 20 candlesticks (ie, 20 working days) the market rallied $10.

Figure 6-5 has a Hammer at the bottom as well, except this is a 10-minute chart. More or less exactly the same thing happened over this 10-minute period as happened on the Hammer day in Chart 6-4: the market sold off and then rallied, closing strongly. The message is the same; there was a period of time where the market sold off then recovered – a sign that the buyers had returned to the fray because the price looked cheap.

The range on this 10-minute period was 17 ticks. The market sold off from 113.77 to 113.63 then rallied to print 113.80 before ending the 10-minute period at 113.78. The following 20 candles (representing 3 hours and 20 minutes of trade) saw the market rally steadily, adding 29 ticks.

Source: CQG, Inc. © 2008 All rights reserved worldwide.

Figure 6-5: Eurex Bund futures; 10-minute candlestick chart; 18 April 2008, 11.20am to 7.20pm

It doesn't matter what the time frame is, the message is the same: the market has witnessed some selling off, but found support and then rallied – the market may have found a bottom.

Now we're getting down to the real crux of the whole thing. Candlesticks tell you where the market has been. From this you can make assumptions as to the state of mind of the market as a whole. You can make up your mind as to whether the bulls are feeling confident or whether they're recovering from a good beating. You can decide whether the bulls are running the show and whether they're comfortable in doing so. You can tell when the cracks are appearing, when things may be changing. It doesn't matter whether this is with respect to short-term time frames or long-term, because the two way pull, the tug-of-war, is dealing with the same issues: fear, greed, emotion, elation, euphoria, crowd psychology, etc etc.

Candlesticks can be an extremely potent ally for short-term time frame traders, and in the many years I've been advising traders on market direction using candlesticks I've almost always done so using 10-minute and 60-minute candle charts for short-term turning points, and daily and weekly charts to keep tabs on overall direction.

Emotion

The key, then, is to work out your time frame. One of the biggest challenges facing any trader is working out the time frame that works for them. We are all individuals, and on that basis will all have different ways of dealing with things. Trading is an emotional game, there's no getting away from it. This is where technical analysis can help, and in particular candlestick analysis, because the signals provided can **reduce** the emotion in your decision making process, whether for trade entry or trade management/exit strategy. I have heard people say that technical analysis can remove the emotion from trading but this is wrong. The vast majority of people cannot remove emotion from trading, but you need to try and find a way to manage it so that the old evil pairing of fear and greed do not take over your decision making. As soon as they take over, you're on a slippery slope.

But there's no point in a day trader using the weekly chart for signals, and by the same token a fund manager has little use for 10-minute charts. I often think that there is a real opportunity for voice brokers with a technical leaning. Longer-term money managers could come up with the ideas, then leave it to the broker to time the entry of the trade using short-term technicals.

Applying flexibility when viewing short-term time frame charts

In the early chapters of this book I covered some of the more popular candlestick reversal patterns, and with each one I presented a box that summarised the rules that need to be satisfied for each particular pattern. Now I'm going to suggest that there are times when the rules need to be, let's say, massaged!

If you are viewing intra-day candlestick charts for liquid products such as, say, S&P 500 futures, do you get gaps between the candles; gaps that are needed to form patterns like Dark Cloud Cover, Stars or Engulfing candles? The answer is no, in the main. Most candlesticks will start exactly at (or at worst a tick away from) the same price as the close of the last candle on intra-day charts, as there is literally a nanosecond between one candle ending and the next one starting. Just because one 10-minute period is over and another is beginning doesn't mean we're suddenly going to see a big jump (or fall) in price. This needs to be factored into the equation.

Look at the following chart. It shows a couple of bottoms on a short-term chart, both of which were very effective, and both of which would have been called Piercing Patterns had there been a gap lower on the first trade of the second candle. But this isn't going to happen in reality on a short-term intra-day chart – the real message is in the strength of the rally on the second candle. We need to adopt a flexible approach to where these candles start life, or we will be missing the patterns, and the message that they're conveying.

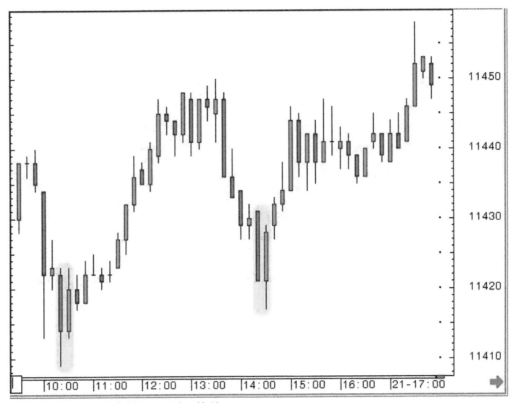

Source: CQG, Inc. © 2008 All rights reserved worldwide.

Figure 6-6: Eurex March 2003 Bund futures; 10-minute candlestick chart; 21 January 2003, 9.30am – 6.00pm

Going through the time frames for trade placement and management

Those looking to put on longer-term trades but searching for the best possible entry, and later on exit, can start with short-term time frames then move up through the time frames until they've got a position on and are looking at a chart that suits the time frame of the trade.

Quite often something like a 10-minute or 30-minute chart can be used to gauge the market's sentiment in the short-term. You may have a big line to buy, but you can see clearly on the short-term charts that the market is coming off, and that there's some strong support just below. You could wait and see if the market reacts to the strong support then jump in as and when bullish reversals appear on the short-term charts at these levels. The fact is you already know you want to buy, you're just asking the chart to show you the best time to do so. If the short-term chart has got you into a trade you can then switch to a longer-term chart to run the trade.

Why do you need to jump to a longer time frame? Because the same short-term chart that gave you those early clues to get in can also spook you to jump out of your position too early. Viewing a 60-minute or daily chart is far less exciting than looking at a 10-minute chart, even though it's tracking the same prices.

As with many things in charting and trading, it's all about the messages that get sent to the brain. A less exciting chart means less chance that you'll trigger some sort of panic mechanism and jump out of your trade early.

If you're in a position for a few days and it's starting to work out well the ideal scenario is to use the weekly chart for stop placement, and to run the thing for as long as possible.

Stop orders

Placement of stops (and subsequently moving stops to protect a profit) is essential for successful trading, and a candlestick chart is as good a canvas as any for this exercise. I also have a lot of time for Point & Figure charts and Ichimoku charts with respect to the running of trailing stops, but that's for another time!

We've spoken about gaps and Marabuzo lines as strong support levels during uptrends and great references as resistance in a market that's heading lower. These could also be incorporated into your stop strategy.

Different time frames all showing reversal patterns = alert!

Earlier we looked at the idea of spotting reversal patterns on weekly and (at the same time) daily charts. This exercise can be just as effective with short-term time frames. Many short-term traders in the futures markets use 10-minute or 15-minute charts, whereas longer-term players will tend to be watching longer-term charts – hourly charts at least. I get very excited when I see candlestick reversal patterns on short-term (say 10-minute) charts that appear at the same time as reversal patterns on the 30-minute or hourly charts. This means that different types of trader are all getting the same message from their candlestick charts, and if everyone starts to pull in the same direction you should start to see a definite one way reaction.

And this sort of situation is not unusual, as I'll try to explain below. Take a combination of three candlesticks on a 10-minute chart that have the look and feel of a Morning Star.

As we've discussed it's very unlikely that the gaps to form a textbook Morning Star will appear on the 10-minute chart, so we need to exercise some flexibility. You can see opposite that the three candles highlighted are a large filled candle, a small-bodied candle flagging indecision, then a big open candle to confirm the turnaround. So the idea of a Morning Star is clear, I hope you agree. Also, in this example the middle candle was a rather neat Doji.

Source: CQG, Inc. © 2008 All rights reserved worldwide.

Figure 6-7: Bund futures (June 2008); 10-minute candlestick chart; 24 April 2008, 5.30pm until 25 April 2008, 2pm

Remember because it is an intra-day chart we're exercising some of that flexibility talked about earlier.

Now let's look at the 30-minute chart (Figure 6-8). You can see a clear Hammer candlestick. Whatever the time frame being viewed the trader is looking at a powerful reversal, because the price action has taken on a "V" shaped direction of travel. The buyers are back!

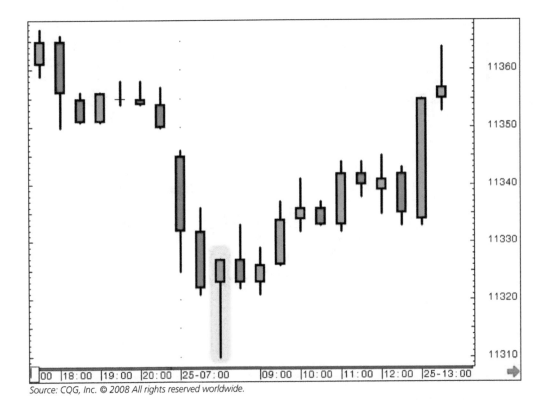

Source: CQG, Inc. © 2008 All rights reserved worldwide.

Figure 6-8: Bund futures (June 2008); 30-minute candlestick chart; 24 April 2008, 5.30pm until 25 April 2008, 2pm

This is another gentle introduction to the idea of merging or blending candles, as Nison calls it. If you have a series of candlesticks that look like they should be a reversal but there's no firm name to attach to them, try moulding them together. You may just find you're staring at a potent pattern like a Hammer or a Shooting Star!

The three candles that form an Evening Star on a 10-minute chart, when combined together, will likely give you a Shooting Star, which is what will be showing up on the 30-minute chart. For a reminder of what I'm talking about here refer back to Figure 4-14.

Which neatly brings us back to our "going through the time frames" idea. Say you've bought something on the back of a Doji on the 10-minute chart. This Doji turned out to be the middle candle of a flexible Morning Star, which blends to form another Hammer on the 30-minute chart. All the time frames are screaming the same thing, and if you've moved up to the 30-minute chart from the 10-minute you will still be confident that a bottom is in place due to the Doji on your chart.

Using candlesticks in conjunction with support and resistance

Using candlestick charts for negative selection

We've touched upon this previously when we talked about the longer-term trader who's looking to enter into a trade, but instead of jumping in with both feet waits to see whether the reversal patterns start to appear when the market gets down to an important support level.

Support and resistance levels are created because markets have a memory, and as a mass we remember where things have got down to previously. Where the buyers returned to the fray last time the market sold off. Where the market turned, and therefore where the buyers decided enough was enough. Or maybe they simply decided that things were just way too cheap!

But if a market gets down to a supposed support level and there's not a sniff of a reversal from the candlesticks, maybe there isn't going to be a reversal, and if we then leave well alone we can save ourselves from a bad trade. The candles have to come to the party as well, and if they don't they can save us from bad trades.

This is what I mean by negative selection. Traditionally we look for candle charts to provide us with tradeable signals. What I'm suggesting here is that they can *stop* you from putting on bad trades.

Support plays

Obviously views can change, but often you find markets bouncing from the same levels that they bounced from the previous hour, day, week, or sometimes even months and years.

You only have to look at the following chart to see a prime example of a market doing exactly that, and it's no coincidence that the reversal patterns also appeared at this time. At the very least this should put you on alert that a change may be occurring.

Source: CQG, Inc. © 2008 All rights reserved worldwide.

Figure 6-9: CME Group Gold futures (unadjusted active continuation); daily candlestick chart; 11 January 2008 – 23 May 2008, showing 17 April 2008 Shooting Star, on former high from 28 March 2008. Then, on 2 May the price got down to the low from 22 January 2008 and a Hammer was posted, which ended that move.

Resistance plays

The same applies to upside levels, or resistance, as it's commonly known. Markets quite often fall over at similar levels to previous failures. Think about the trader who was long last time the market went up to £20 but didn't get out. He or she was still long when prices went back down to £15, and given a second chance – if prices get back to £20 again – the trader may well take his or her money and run. Think about the trader who wants to buy some but has seen that £20 has been a barrier previously. Maybe they'll hold off until this hurdle is clear. The speculator trading via a spread bet or CFD has the opportunity to go short and may feel that this one's ripe to fall over again on reaching the £20 mark. All of these factors would contribute to either a splurge of selling, or a dearth of buying, as prices approach £20. Supply and demand tells us that this will result in lower prices as the market has to head lower to look for keen buyers. If there are more sellers than buyers the price has to go down...

If you get to a resistance level and reversal patterns start to appear you should be ready for a turnaround, as shown in the example of the Shooting Star in Figure 6-9.

Figure 6.10 shows gold failing at 875 on 21 January 1980, then topping out at 729 on a renewed move higher on 11 February 1980, and then again months later on 23 September 1980.

I think you'll agree that 729 was a big level at this time.

Source: CQG, Inc. © 2008 All rights reserved worldwide.

Figure 6-10: COMEX Gold futures (unadjusted active continuation); weekly candlestick chart; November 1979 – February 1982

Then have a look at the following chart, Figure 6-11. Two Shooting Star candlesticks appeared in gold futures in May 2006, just when prices got back to the 26-year-old level of 729. Within days trading had changed tack and I was looking for a pullback, which duly came.

Source: CQG, Inc. © 2008 All rights reserved worldwide.

Figure 6-11: CME Group Gold futures (unadjusted active continuation); daily candlestick chart; 24 March 2006 – 16 June 2006

I've reproduced this chart many times; it's one of my old favourites, and I've been challenged a few times that if you had adjusted for inflation then gold would need to get up to somewhere north of $2000 in 2006 to be anywhere near its 1981 levels in real terms. I don't dispute this, but you also can't ignore the fact that by drawing a horizontal line on the chart you would have been (and I was), at the very least aware of this level, and could have taken profit on longs somewhere near the high of the move.

A Shooting Star bang on a massive resistance level will surely carry more weight than a reversal signal that just appears out of the middle of nowhere?

At the time that these two Shooting Star candles appeared it was difficult to think about the idea of batting against such a solid trend, and looking back at my analysis at this time I didn't change tack fully to the bear side until the market sold off through 650. At this time I targeted 550, a long-term Fibonacci retracement level that was reached a few weeks later.

Waiting for confirmation – what to use

So this is how I do it: I'm always watching keenly for candlestick reversal patterns, and then when I see one I do absolutely nothing, preferring to wait for some confirmation before jumping on the reversal bandwagon. This is the result of years of experience – years of jumping too early!

This is where trend lines, moving averages, Fibonacci levels, gaps, Marabuzo lines and the like come into play. Upon seeing a reversal pattern in a rising market we immediately look for the first significant support level and we ask that it gets broken to confirm the reversal. Prior to this some lightening up of longs may be advisable, but an all out bear tack needs a bit more time to be decided upon.

Likewise, if the market is in a downtrend and a reversal pattern appears, we immediately look up and find the first strong resistance level. We want to see the market through here at the very least before we think about buying.

A few more practical examples of support and resistance combining well with candlesticks, over various time frames, can be seen in the following charts.

Examples

The following chart illustrates how you can use candlesticks with support and resistance to place short-term trades that can make a quick profit and involve minimal risk.

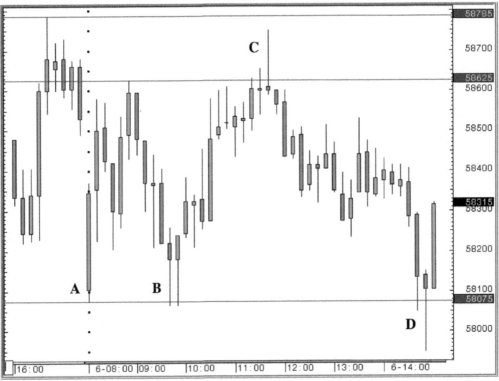

Source: CQG, Inc. © 2008 All rights reserved worldwide.

Figure 6-12: LIFFE FTSE futures (March 2008); 10-minute candlestick chart; 4.00pm, 5 February 2008 – 3.10pm, 6 February 2008

Point A is the start of trade on 6 February. The first hour sees a range set of 5807.5 to 5862.5. It didn't quite reach the first resistance from the previous day at 5878.5. Then the market sold off to point B, which saw the low from earlier in the day retested. Prices held this level, and a Hammer was posted to boot. In fact two were posted in a row. Combined with the hold of support this would have seen day traders buying. They would have made money trading on the bull side right up until the Shooting Star at point C was reached. This appeared when a high of 5875 was set, slightly above the 5862.5 high set in the first hour, but just below the 5878.5 high from late in the session on 5 February.

If you had taken this Shooting Star at resistance as a sell signal you would have traded to the short side from then on, until Point D was reached. The market got through the earlier lows, only to retake these levels very quickly, ending that 10-minute period with a Hammer, which would have flipped you back to the buy side. Again there would have been some instant gratification for longs after this pattern.

You didn't need to be a bull or a bear to make money using these parameters. You didn't need a directional view at all.

All you needed was a flexible approach to trading, tight stop criteria and discipline, and a keen eye for candlestick patterns coinciding with technical levels. This is a mistake I often make, as many traders do. I was bearish about the markets on this particular day, so would have favoured the sell trade after the Shooting Star, and would have missed the Hammer opportunities. My being "married to the bear tack" would have stopped me making money from the well flagged short-term up moves.

Some would argue this is no bad thing, though, since the market was in a pretty beaten up state around this time, and there was quite a bit of risk attached to trading on the long side. These are valid arguments, and decisions will depend on several factors, including time frames, expectations from trades, risk versus reward and running tight stops, all of which are beyond the scope of this introductory book.

Source: CQG, Inc. © 2008 All rights reserved worldwide.

Figure 6-13: Eurex Bobl futures (adjusted active continuation); daily candlestick chart; 11 February 2008 – 23 April 2008

We have shown this chart before. We talked about it in Chapter 3 (Figure 3-22). The candle at the very top of this chart is a Rickshaw Man. As you can see this pattern appeared on the day the market retested the high from a few days earlier. At the time that the market got above that previous high, the bulls were in charge and looking good for it. But they dropped the ball, and prices ended up back where they started. The market started selling off from the very next day as the bears picked up the ball and started running back up the other end with it!

Combining candles with momentum studies

When I spend a good amount of time with a group of trainees the thing I try to impress upon them is that they are all individuals and that they're all going to find different things that work well for them as individuals from the huge array of technical tools available. I'm even happy to concede that they might choose not to use technicals at all, although I say this through gritted teeth!

Work out your favoured canvas

My best suggestion is to work out what your favourite canvas is. Some swear by Market Profile charts, some see Point & Figure as the cleanest and clearest way of viewing the markets and gleaning signals. Some will firmly stick to bar charts even after reading this book, I guess (astonishing!)

Whatever you decide, there's more to do once this decision has been reached. We've talked about waiting for confirmation before taking a reversal signal in the previous chapter, but there are other methods that can be employed for confirmation purposes. A reliable moving average, a trend line, or a signal from an indicator like Stochastics or RSI are the sort of thing that you can incorporate into your decision making process.

It comes back to the analogy I used earlier: if you wake up one morning and decide to buy a red jumper do you go to the high street and buy the very first red jumper you clap your eyes on, or do you have a few more criteria you want to satisfy? On something as simple as buying a pullover you've got more than one condition, and you need to have layers of conditions that need satisfying before jumping into a trade.

Over the following pages you will see the same chart reproduced several times, each time with a different method of confirmation used. I have accompanied each chart with a brief explanation of the method. This is by no means a definitive discussion, more a précis of each method, with enough to help you decide whether it's something you might attempt to incorporate into your strategy.

Support and resistance

This is a recap of the previous section but it fits in nicely with what I'm trying to do in this section, so here goes!

Support occurs when a market that is selling off reaches a level where the buyers return to the fray sufficiently to turn things around. Using the basic laws of supply and demand we know that a market that is selling off is the result of more sellers than buyers. Supply is outstripping demand. But the moment when price reverses and the market starts to go up is where the balance between buyers and sellers changes.

It is often noted that markets change from downwards to upwards at similar levels to previously, so chartists look back at the historic prices to see where previous turning points occurred.

Resistance is the opposite to support: a high price where the balance between buyers and sellers shifts back in favour of the sellers. In an uptrending market the bulls, or buyers, are dominating. The top of a move is when the sellers take over, where demand no longer outstrips supply, causing a top in price. Previous highs are well watched levels when a market is rising. These levels are the moments at which market conditions changed previously, where the balance of power changed from bulls to bears. It's obvious why they are classed as so important.

To take support and resistance one very simple step further, many chartists and traders look for a clearly defined trend whenever they fire up a chart. Charles Dow first mooted the simple idea that an uptrend is a series of higher highs and higher lows, whereas a downtrend is comprised of lower highs and lower lows.

Source: CQG, Inc. © 2008 All rights reserved worldwide.

Figure 6-14: CME Group mini-Dow futures (unadjusted active continuation); daily candlestick chart with support and resistance lines; 7 March 2007 – 8 June 2007

Using this basic assumption on the preceding chart, you can see where the uptrend started (hence giving us a buy signal), and where the market broke a previous higher low to stop the long trade out. On this occasion the lower lows and lower highs were not really clearly defined when we got out of the trade, but things had started to look messy and the price had broken an important support, thus triggering liquidation of the long position.

Moving averages

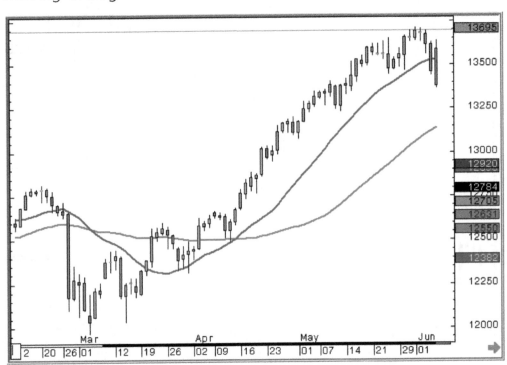

Source: CQG, Inc. © 2008 All rights reserved worldwide.

Figure 6-15: CME Group mini-Dow futures (unadjusted active continuation); daily candlestick chart with 20 and 50-day simple moving averages; 7 March 2007 – 7 June 2007

Many traders and analysts use a moving average line as a reference for market direction, as it smoothes the data set. Sometimes candlesticks can be a tad confusing and trends can be difficult to define. A moving average takes the average value of a set amount of data (usually closes) and plots them as a line. They are called moving averages because the lines move with the market. A 10-day moving average adds up the last ten days of data and divides the total by ten. Obviously as a new candlestick is added to the right hand side of the chart we lose one from 11 days before from our calculation. Hence the line moves with the movement of the candlesticks.

The preceding chart – Figure 6-15 – is a daily candle chart with 20-day and 50-day simple moving averages applied. Note particularly how the 20-day line reacts more quickly to the price trend changing than the 50-day average.

Also see how on several occasions we saw a pullback in the uptrend that got prices down to the 20-day average line.

So if after the Evening Star in early March and the Hammer in mid-March (the bottom left hand side of the chart – there should be no need to highlight them by now), you ask for a break of the 20-day moving average to confirm, you got your confirmation on 20 March and bought at 12,381. If you subsequently used the same 20-day moving average line as a trailing stop you would have been at most 66 ticks offside on 30 March, and you would have sold out for a profit of 1080 points on the close on the 6 June.

A simple rule of thumb if you want to apply moving averages to candlesticks is to use your eyes, and find the average line (by playing around with different period settings) that acts as good support in a rising market (ie, any pullbacks in the uptrend find a bottom at or around the moving average line), and good resistance (ie, it caps upside advances) in a falling market. Then you want to see that it gives clear signals when the market crosses the line.

This all sounds easy but it isn't, and a lot of patience and time is required to find the line that does the best job for you. One of the biggest problems with moving averages is that they become rather unreliable during trendless or sideways markets, so this is something to watch out for and guard against when you're backtesting.

Trend lines

Source: CQG, Inc. © 2008 All rights reserved worldwide.

Figure 6-16: CME Group mini-Dow futures (unadjusted active continuation); daily candlestick chart with trend lines; 7 March 2007 – 8 June 2007

Trend lines are straight lines that define trends. It is amazing how many times the market moves higher or lower with a consistently steady velocity that can be tracked by a straight line.

An uptrend line is a straight line that joins a series of higher lows in a market that is travelling higher. You draw them below the price action, sloping higher from left to right. You can use them to define the move and keep you in a long trade. You can put a trailing stop below a trend line, and your stop order will move higher as the market moves higher.

A downtrend line is a straight line that sits above a downtrending market, joining successive lower highs.

I always apply a "rule of three" to the drawing of trend lines. I want to see three lower highs joined together before classing a line as a hard and fast downtrend line.

A move up to a downtrend line where a bearish reversal pattern is posted is a good start for a short trade set up. Once in the trade, as long as the market moves back down, away from the line, you can use the line as a reference for a trailing stop.

If you have three higher lows that can be joined with a straight line you have a valid uptrend support line and you should be looking to buy dips to this line, especially if the market displays bullish candlesticks when hitting the line.

Using the same chart as before we can see that in this case the short-term downtrend line was broken after the candlestick reversal patterns, but just prior to our moving average buy signal. The exit was a few days later than the moving average sell signal, but at similar levels. The main message was that the trailing stop using the trend line kept you in the trade for a good while.

Parabolic SAR

Source: CQG, Inc. © 2008 All rights reserved worldwide.

Figure 6-17: CME Group mini-Dow futures (unadjusted active continuation); daily candlestick chart with Parabolic SAR; 7 March 2007 – 8 June 2007

This is a study devised by Welles Wilder and introduced in his 1978 book *New Concepts in Technical Trading Systems*. It relies on a trailing stop that gets closer to the action as the trend progresses. As you can see, trades are triggered when prices move through the dashes in one direction or the other.

It is an "always in" trading tool, which means you are either short or long at all times. SAR stands for Stop and Reverse, ie, you stop out the previous position, and simultaneously move to the opposite tack. I don't tend to use it quite so literally. I find it can be good to keep you in a strong trend for as long as possible. It is another effective tool for stop placement, and for giving trend beginning and trend ending signals, but as with a moving average it can be a rather unreliable tool during sideways markets.

Once again we've kept the same chart for this as the previous examples of moving averages and trend lines. We got an earlier signal, and this would have actually seen you quite a bit offside before things came good. In this instance the SAR dashes didn't do the best job for us, although you can see how they can have value in strongly trending conditions.

MACD

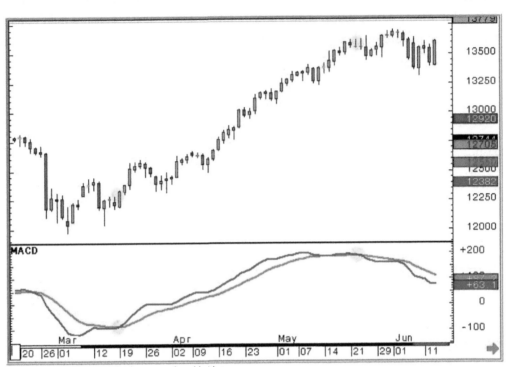

Source: CQG, Inc. © 2008 All rights reserved worldwide.

Figure 6-18: CME Group mini-Dow futures (unadjusted active continuation); daily candlestick chart with MACD (12,26,9); 7 March 2007 – 8 June 2007

MACD stands for moving average convergence/divergence and is a momentum study that gives clear-cut buy and sell signals with the crossing of two lines, one of which is a moving average of the other. The faster base line (the blue line in this example) tracks the difference between two moving averages (the default being the 12 and 26 day exponential moving averages). Longer-term traders find this a robust, reliable momentum study. Once you've seen a candlestick reversal pattern you want to add weight to the argument for a reversal, and a corresponding signal from something like MACD is a good example of the sort of thing you may want to add into your check box system.

You can see once more that after our reversal patterns we get a buy signal from the crossing of the MACD lines, and once the market starts to fall over so do the lines, leading to a sell signal which came slightly earlier than those seen so far from trend lines, moving averages and the like.

RSI

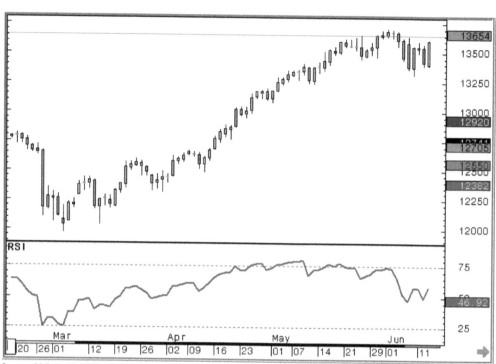

Source: CQG, Inc. © 2008 All rights reserved worldwide.

Figure 6-19: CME Group mini-Dow futures (unadjusted active continuation); daily candlestick chart with RSI (14 day); 7 March 2007 – 8 June 2007

This is a momentum study dealing with the ratio of up days to down days over a set time period. It is constructed only using one line, which generally moves in the same direction as the market. Many traders look for Divergence set ups, where the indicator goes in one direction and the market in another; these can work extremely well combined with candlestick analysis, with one signal confirming the other. One of my favourite momentum studies, and well worth reading up on (once again this was introduced by J Welles Wilder in *New Concepts in Technical Trading Systems*)!

As you can see, throughout most of May the market kept heading higher but the RSI had topped out a lot earlier, and didn't subsequently emulate this high. Even a month later in July, the indicator failed to follow when the Dow rallied to new highs before finally topping out and cracking nastily lower as the 2007 sub-prime crisis bit hard.

Stochastics

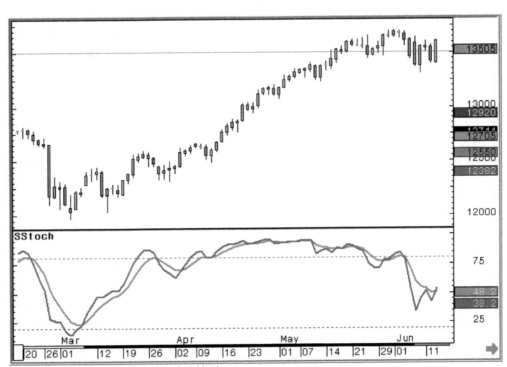

Source: CQG, Inc. © 2008 All rights reserved worldwide.

Figure 6-20: CME Group mini-Dow futures (unadjusted active continuation); daily candlestick chart with Slow Stochastics (10,3,3); 7 March 2007 – 8 June 2007

The Stochastic Oscillator has a similar interpretation to MACD and RSI. This short-term momentum study employs two lines, with the crossing of the lines giving definitive buy and sell signals. Once again you can use something like a Stochastics signal as confirmation for any candlestick reversal pattern.

A classic buy signal is the lines coming out of oversold (ie, from below a reading of 20) then crossing, with the blue line piercing through the red line. As you can see this gave a pretty early signal in this instance, hard on the heels of the Morning Star formation, but as with the Parabolic SAR discussed earlier there was a fair bit of draw down after the signal was given before the Hammer was posted and the market got going to the upside once more.

The other thing this chart shows well is how unreliable signals can be from a short-term momentum study when a market is in a solid trend, but as with the RSI a divergence set-up came to the rescue to try and make sense of things. If this had caused you to liquidate longs you would have missed the last month of the bull move, but you would not have been long when things started selling off hard soon after that.

So what to use?

One thing that the past few pages may have had you thinking is that across all the different methods discussed we ended up with pretty similar confirmation signals, and pretty similar exits. I did this deliberately, with a familiar and constant chart; to try and get you thinking. This won't always be the case, and there will be certain indicators or methods that work better for you than others. Your job is to discover what works best for you on your charts, taking into account your time frame and your style of trading.

In other words, you need to work it out and decide!

Tick the boxes

I encourage the idea of producing, at least in the early days, a grid where you need to tick say four boxes before pulling the trigger. Below is an example:

Conditions for a buy signal

Established long/medium term uptrend	Y/N
Retracement sell off seen on light volume	Y/N
Bullish candlestick reversal pattern after pullback	Y/N
Now rallying, and breaks first strong resistance	Y/N
Buy signal from Slow Stochastics	Y/N
Pick up in volume as buyers return	Y/N

If most of the answers are "Yes," then you have a compelling argument that the selling is done and you should be getting long...

After a while this way of systemising your trading decisions will become second nature, but even then if you find yourself starting to make undisciplined "hope" trades, you can go back to using this sort of grid in order to force yourself to justify your decisions.

Once you're in, stay in!

One other idea I would also like to try and encourage you to think about is that you will probably need something else to keep you in a winning trade for as long as possible, but which will get you out in a timely fashion. It's an easy trap to fall into to use the same thing for entry and exit, but I don't think that's necessarily the way forward.

Obviously using the example grid on the previous page, you could argue that you get out of a long position once you tick all the boxes that are saying you should sell, but I'm not sure it's as simple as that. I like to find a way to use a trailing stop once you're in a trade, and obvious candidates to achieve this result are moving averages, trend lines, or one of my favourites: Welles Wilder's Parabolic SAR.

I also like using Marabuzo lines for this, as you can see from Figure 6-21. At the bottom is a Hammer on a strong support. The market then starts to move higher in an obvious uptrend, and we were able to stay bullish all the way up in this one, and use Marabuzo lines as a reference to stay with the bulls every time they appeared. The trend was extremely strong during this period, and the lines all pretty much held like a dream. Sweet!

Source: CQG, Inc. © 2008 All rights reserved worldwide.

Figure 6-21: ICE Gas Oil futures (unadjusted active continuation); daily candlestick chart; 14 November 2007 – 27 March 2008

There's a load more on this chart as well, though. Have you spotted the variation on an Evening Star at key resistance at the start of January? Or the Hammer on support towards the end of January? How about the Inverted Hammer that was confirmed the following day just a few weeks later? Not the strongest of patterns, until the market gapped higher the next day. Then the market got through the previous resistance and posted a nice big reaction day in mid-February. There was no stopping the market then, not until prices got up to the psychologically important $1000 mark. The day this level was hit a Shooting Star was posted. Then traders sold off, but only to a Marabuzo line, where a small bodied candlestick was posted upon hitting this key support.

I could point all of these out to you, but we're at the end of the book, and I'm rather hoping you're finding them yourself now!

Chapter summary

A lot of time and energy is spent on momentum indicators these days, among both professional and beginner traders. I always beg newcomers not to get too bogged down with these, and to make sure they don't have too many indicators all running alongside each other, as they will often be telling you the same thing.

"Paralysis by analysis" is a phrase that springs to mind.

But even saying that, an indicator can be an integral element of a trading system, and there's **nothing more important than having a system.**

I'm a big believer that candlesticks can be incorporated into any trading system, and can enhance your system, for example by providing an earlier "heads up" indication of trend change.

7

Summing Up

I've done a lot of summing up in the previous two chapters, because once you've trawled through the patterns and you understand the psychology behind them the main thing to do is to try and apply it in real life. It's a criticism that I've often seen levelled at the technical analysis community: that it all reads well but how am I going to use it?

Hopefully you are now empowered sufficiently to feel that it is something worth trying out!

The best way I can sum up this book is to say this: hopefully you don't see a candlestick chart as a "one stop shop" signal-generating tool. It's not just there to be a robot, chucking out buy and sell signals. It's not as simple as that, I'm afraid. It tells you where the market has been and whether this is the result of strong buying or selling, or a change of balance between these two conditions.

You need to treat it as such; it's telling you where a market has been, and if you know what's been going on up until the present, you can at the very least have an idea as to where things may go in the future. If the Australian cricket team have won 18 out of their last 20 test matches there's a good chance they'll do well in the next Ashes series, no? (Unfortunately!)

I find it incredible that traders and money managers can make decisions on a stock or a market without considering the sentiment in the market at the time, and I strongly believe that a chart, especially a candlestick chart, is one of the best ways to get a snapshot of sentiment, and any changes that may be occurring as far as the balance of bulls and bears is concerned.

I said at the very beginning of this book that my ideal reader is someone who is a cynic of technical analysis, and my hope is that this book will have converted them.

The tongue was in the cheek a bit when I wrote this. What I really hope is that the biggest cynics out there will at least identify that there's some value in gauging market sentiment, and that candlestick analysis can do this as well as anything.

Good luck with whatever you're doing in the markets, and hopefully candlesticks will now be a part of that!

8

Ten Golden Rules When Trading Using Candlesticks

1. **Never use candlestick charts to bat against established, obvious trends.** Some people like to use a chart as a way of backing up their view of a particular stock or market. You need to be totally objective when viewing charts. I have worked with people before who have asked me to look at charts for this and that. I've always requested that they don't tell me what their view is at this point. I prefer the question "What do you think of Vodafone?" rather than "I think Vodafone is going up, what does the chart say?" I'm a big believer that the best traders and money managers in the world have a strong fundamental background and they use technicals to back this up and to help them time their trades. If they believe something's undervalued and should go up they wait until the chart agrees!

2. **Never use candlesticks in isolation.** I think this has been drummed home enough in the last few chapters; you need to combine candlesticks with at least one method of confirmation. Using candles on their own is unlikely to reap rewards.

3. **Don't restrict yourself to one time frame.** You can get different information from different time frame charts, and it adds an extra dimension to your reading of the markets. Short-term time frames can be good for entering into trades, while longer-

term time frames can remove the apparent volatility from your viewing of the chart once you're in a position.

4. **Remember your support and resistance levels.** Looking for candlestick reversal patterns at former highs and lows, or near to an important level like a well watched moving average, can be extremely effective.

5. **Do your homework and find the patterns that work well for the chart you use.** If Shooting Stars have hardly ever worked in the past on your chart, it's probable that that poor run will continue – so don't use them as reversal signals! Backtesting is so important when you're searching for the candlesticks worth looking out for on your charts.

6. **Don't kid yourself when backtesting.** There's nothing worse than thinking you've got the best system in the world, then finding out once you're putting your money where your mouth is that you messed up when backtesting because you weren't honest about entry and exit points. A "worst case scenario" approach towards where you get in and out of trades serves one well as this should mean results actually improve in the real world.

7. **Don't enter into a trade without knowing where your stop is.** I've seen this in many a "trading rules" list. It's nothing new, and it's essential! Having a stop is paramount in trading. Hopefully you can move your stop after a short time, so it's no longer a Stop Loss but becomes a Stop Profit! I recommend you try to develop a trailing stop strategy.

8. **Refer to the "Cheat Sheet" regularly until you've learnt the patterns off by heart.** This will save you from continually having to flick through the book.

9. **Don't bother with bar charts ever again.** Why would you want to look at bar charts when the candle chart can add so much extra information even at the first glance?

10. **Always make sure you look at the candlestick chart in future when checking out a stock or a market.** Even if you don't want to learn the patterns (see rule number 8), surely you're now going to afford yourself a brief glance at a chart from now on every time you're thinking of doing something in the market. The chart can quickly give you an idea of the market's overall thinking, and you can stop yourself from batting against an obvious trend.

Index

A

Abandoned Baby candle 103

B

backtesting 28, 29, 122, 151, 166
       realistic testing 44
bar chart 2, 3, 4, 63, 147, 166
bearish continuation patterns, see candlesticks, patterns
bearish outside day 72, 74
bearish reversal patterns, see candlesticks, patterns
broker's commission 44
bullish continuation patterns, see candlesticks, patterns
bullish reversal pattern, see candlesticks, patterns
buy signal, conditions to meet 159

C

candlesticks
       benefits of 9

S

SAR, see Stop and Reverse pattern

shadow 8, 16, 67, 81, 90

    definition 7

    Gravestone Doji 53

    Hammer 20, 32, 33

    Hanging Man 47, 48

    Inverted Hammer 42, 45

    Shooting Star 34, 35, 37, 38, 41

    shadow line 8

Shooting Star, see candlesticks, patterns, bearish reversal patterns

slippage 44

Society of Technical Analysts, The xi

Stochastic Oscillator 158

Stop and Reverse pattern 154

    trailing stops, useful for 160

stop loss, see stop orders

stop orders 124, 152, 166

    essential for successful trading 135

supply and demand 5, 9, 141, 148

support levels 28, 30, 67, 73, 118, 120, 125, 139, 143

    Marabuzo lines 113-114, 125

T

technical analysis v, vii, ix, 9, 10, 13, 26, 41, 80, 93, 128, 130, 163, 164

    managing emotion while trading 133

time frames 43, 135

    agreement between 136, 138, 165

    candlesticks, applicable in all 67

U

V

W

Candlesticks Cheat Sheet

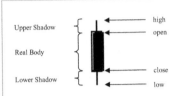

Japanese candlesticks are constructed using the open, high, low and close prices of the timeframe specified. The difference between the open and close gives us the "Real Body". The extremes of the day give us the "tails" or "wicks" of the candle, known as the upper and lower shadows.

Bullish Marabuzo
Bullish: Big range day where the market opened near the low and closed near the high. The Bulls were in charge for the majority of the session.

Bearish Marabuzo
Bearish: Big range day where the market opened near the high and closed near its lows. The Bears were in charge for the majority of the session.

Shooting Star
Bearish when seen in an uptrend. The upper shadow is at least twice the length of the real body, which is at the bottom of the day's range.

Hammer
Bullish reversal signal if it comes in a downtrend, it indicates that the market is "hammering out" a bottom. The lower shadow must be at least twice the length of the short real body – which is at the top of the candle's range.

Inverted Hammer
A Bullish pattern if seen in a downtrend. Requires confirmation as it's not generally the strongest of signals.

Hanging Man
The same shape as a Hammer but Bearish in an uptrend. This also needs further confirmation.

Doji
Indecision: The open and close at the same level proves that buyers and sellers are balancing each other out. Signals a reversal if seen in a solid up or down trend.

Bullish Harami

A small open real body contained within the previous day's filled real body signals a reversal when seen in a downtrend. Not generally a strong signal.

Bearish Harami
The opposite to a Bullish Harami. A two candle pattern in an uptrend where the second, filled real body is small and contained within the open real body of the first candlestick. Not a strong reversal signal.

Bullish Engulfing Pattern
Bullish if seen during a downtrend. The second open/white candle must totally envelop the real body of the first.

Bearish Engulfing Pattern
Bearish when you're in an uptrend. The real body of the second filled/dark candle engulfs the real body of the first. A strong reversal signal especially if there is better volume on the second day.

Piercing Pattern
Bullish if seen during a downtrend. Gaps lower on the second day, then rallies strongly into the close. Has to close above the first candle's real body midpoint.

Dark Cloud Cover
Bearish if seen during an uptrend. Gaps higher on the second day, then sells off heavily into the close. Has to close below the first candle's real body midpoint.

Morning Star

A significant reversal if seen in a downtrend. It has three candles, the first two are a "Star", the third confirms, closing well into the real body of the first candle.

Evening Star
An important Bearish Pattern if seen in an uptrend. The middle candle has a small real body which gaps away from the first. The third candle confirms the change of sentiment.

Lightning Source UK Ltd.
Milton Keynes UK
UKOW07f1708241116

288446UK00006B/73/P